DATE DUE 4/18

DISCARD

PRINTED IN U.S.A.

World War II Propaganda

World War II Propaganda

Analyzing the Art of Persuasion during Wartime

DAVID WELCH

ABC-CLIO™

An Imprint of ABC-CLIO, LLC
Santa Barbara, California • Denver, Colorado

Library of Congress Cataloging-in-Publication Data

Names: Welch, David, 1950- author.
Title: World War II propaganda : analyzing the art of persuasion
    during wartime / David Welch.
Other titles: World War Two propaganda
Description: Santa Barbara, California : ABC-CLIO, 2017. | Includes
    bibliographical references and index.
Identifiers: LCCN 2017035827 (print) | LCCN 2017036692 (ebook) |
    ISBN 9781610696746 (ebook) | ISBN 9781610696739 (alk. paper)
Subjects: LCSH: World War, 1939-1945—Propaganda. | Propaganda—
    History—20th century.
Classification: LCC D810.P6 (ebook) | LCC D810.P6 W45 2017 (print) |
    DDC 940.54/88—dc23
LC record available at https://lccn.loc.gov/2017035827

ISBN: 978-1-61069-673-9
EISBN: 978-1-61069-674-6

21 20 19 18 17   1 2 3 4 5

This book is also available as an eBook.

ABC-CLIO
An Imprint of ABC-CLIO, LLC

ABC-CLIO, LLC
130 Cremona Drive, P.O. Box 1911
Santa Barbara, California 93116–1911
www.abc-clio.com

This book is printed on acid-free paper ∞

Manufactured in the United States of America

Contents

Primary Sources

Introduction

The truth, nothing but the truth and, as near as possible, the whole truth.
—*Sir John Reith (British Minister of Information, 1940)*

Propaganda is invariably associated with solely pejorative associations. The word often implies something sinister—synonyms frequently include "lies," "deceit," and "brainwashing." Although propaganda is thousands of years old, it came of age in the 20th century. The development of mass and multimedia offered a fertile ground for propaganda, and the century's global conflicts provided the impetus needed for its growth. As electorates and audiences have become more sophisticated, they have begun to question the use of propaganda in history and its role in contemporary society. However, "propaganda" has become a portmanteau word, which can be interpreted in a number of different ways. Despite the controversy over definition, the subject continues to grow and attract widespread interest. With rapidly changing technology, definitions of propaganda have also undergone changes.

Propaganda has meant different things at different times, although clearly the scale on which it has been practiced has increased in the 20th century. What are the characteristic features of propaganda, and how can it be defined? The origin of the word "propaganda" can be traced back to the Reformation, when the spiritual and ecclesiastic unity of Europe was shattered, and the medieval Roman Church lost its hold on the Northern countries. During the ensuring struggle between forces of Protestantism and those of the counter-Reformation, the Roman Catholic Church found itself faced with the problem of maintaining and strengthening its hold in the non-Catholic countries. A Commission of Cardinals was set up by Gregory XIII (1572–1585) was charged with spreading Catholicism and regulating ecclesiastical affairs in heathen lands. A generation later, when the Thirty Years War had broken out, Gregory XV in 1622 made the commission permanent, as the *Sacra Congregatio de propaganda fide* (Congregation for the Propagation of the Faith); it was charged with the management of foreign missions and financed by a "ring tax" assessed on each newly appointed cardinal. Finally, in 1627, Urban VII established the *Collegium Urbanum* or College of Propaganda to serve as a training ground for a new generation of Catholic propagandists and to educate young priests who were to undertake such missions. The first propagandist institute was, therefore, simply a body charged with improving the dissemination of a group of religious dogmas. The word "propaganda" soon came to be applied to any organization set up for the purpose of spreading a doctrine; subsequently, it was applied to the doctrine itself, and lastly to the methods employed in undertaking the dissemination.[1]

Between the 17th and 20th centuries, we hear comparatively little about "propaganda" as a term. It had but a limited use and, though ill-flavored, was largely unfamiliar. During the English Civil Wars (1642–1651) and the breakdown of the censorship and licensing system established under the Tudors and early Stuarts, propaganda by pamphlet and newsletter became a regular accessory to military action, Oliver Cromwell's Parliamentarian army being concerned nearly as much with the spread of radical religious and political doctrines as with victory in the field.

The employment of propaganda increased steadily throughout the 18th and 19th centuries, particularly at times of ideological struggle, as in the American Revolutionary War (War of Independence; 1775–1783) and the French Revolutionary Wars (1792–1802). From the end of the Napoleonic Wars to the outbreak of World War I in 1914, Europe witnessed many changes. They included a range of smaller revolutionary and independence struggles, the unification of a powerful new Prussian-led Germany (which defeated and humiliated France in 1870), and the emergence of simmering tensions in the Balkans as the weakening Ottoman Empire retreated to the edges of Europe. But there were no great wars of revolution on a French or American scale.

Industrialization, too, played its part now in the advance of propaganda. In the most advanced societies, large and growing print circulations, during the late 18th and 19th centuries, together with improving literacy created new audiences for messages of all kinds. As consumer societies developed, so did a demand for greater political and economic rights—fertile territory for propaganda. Historically, modern propaganda can be seen as a product of post-industrialization when an increasingly literate public become consumers and demand greater political and economic rights. But equally, propaganda was associated with periods of stress and turmoil during which violent controversy over doctrine accompanied the use of force. In the struggle for power, propaganda is an instrument to be used by those who want to secure or retain power just as much as by those wanting to displace them. The relationship between propaganda and war is the theme that binds this book together. Since the late 19th century, war propaganda and the mass media have undergone a long, intricate relationship. Indeed, the history of changing communication technology is often pegged to certain conflicts.

The use of war propaganda dates back 2,400 years to the Chinese general Sun Tzu's *The Art of War*. Sun Tzu, writing around the late sixth century BC, knew all about the power of persuasion: "For to win one hundred victories in one hundred battles is not the acme of skill. To subdue the enemy without fighting is the acme of skill." World War I, however, marked a decisive turning point in the use made of state-sponsored propaganda. The Great War witnessed its first use by governments in an organized, quasi-scientific manner. As a result, between 1914 and 1918, the wholesale employment of propaganda as a weapon of modern warfare served to transform its meaning into something more sinister. Toward the end of the 19th century, the introduction of new forms of communication had created a new historical phenomenon, the mass audience. The means now existed for governments to mobilize entire industrial societies for warfare, to disseminate information (or propaganda) to large groups of people within relatively short time spans. One of the most significant lessons to be learned from the experience of World War I was that public opinion could no longer be ignored as a determining factor in the formulation of government policies. Unlike previous wars, the Great War was the first "total war" in which whole nations, and not just professional armies, were locked in mortal combat. Propaganda was an essential part of this war effort, developing in all the belligerent countries as the war progressed. "Total war" can be defined as warfare in which vast human, material, and emotional resources were marshaled to support military effort. World War I served to increase the level of popular interest and participation in the affairs of state. The gap between the soldier at the front and civilian at home was narrowed substantially in that the entire resources of the state; military, economic, cultural, and psychological had to be mobilized to the full in a fight to the finish. The "ordeal" of total war required that civilians must also "fall-in" and participate (and possibly suffer) in the war effort. In such a struggle, morale came to be recognized as a significant military factor and propaganda emerged as the principle instrument of control over public opinion and an essential weapon in the national arsenal.[2]

After the war, in contrast with the war experience itself, a deep mistrust developed on the part of ordinary British citizens, who concluded that conditions at the front had been deliberately obscured by patriotic slogans and by atrocity propaganda based on obscene stereotypes of the enemy. The population also felt cheated that their sacrifices had not resulted in the promised homes and a land "fit for heroes," as promised by Prime Minister Lloyd George in a speech of November 1918. Propaganda was now associated with lies and falsehood. Even politicians were sensitive to these criticisms and as a result the Ministry of Information (MOI), which had been established to centralize British propaganda in early 1918, was immediately disbanded. Following the end of the conflict, the British government regarded propaganda as politically dangerous and even morally unacceptable in peacetime. Indeed, the impact of propaganda on political behavior had such a profound effect that in World War II, when the British government attempted to educate the population about the existence of Nazi extermination camps, it was not immediately believed. A similar reaction against what was interpreted as propaganda took root in the United States in the wake of the wartime experience. In 1920, George Creel, director of the Committee on Public Information (CPI), which had been set up to "sell the war to the American people," published an account of his achievements as director of the CPI, and in so doing contributed to the public's growing suspicion of propaganda. This atmosphere created a major obstacle for propagandists attempting to rally American support against fascism in the late 1930s and 1940s.

Fledgling dictators in interwar Europe, however, viewed the propaganda of World War I in a very different light. The perceived success of British propaganda provided the defeated Germans with a fertile source of counter-propaganda aimed at the postwar peace treaties and the ignominy of the Weimar Republic that followed the toppling of the Kaiser. Writing in *Mein Kampf*, Adolf Hitler devoted two chapters to propaganda. By maintaining that the German army had not been defeated in battle but had been forced to submit because of disintegration of morale from within German society, accelerated by skillful British propaganda, Hitler—like other right-wing politicians and military groups—was providing historical legitimacy for the "stab-in-the-back" theory. Regardless of the *actual* role played by British (or Soviet) propaganda in helping to bring Germany to its knees, it was generally accepted that Britain's wartime experiment was the ideal blueprint on which other governments might subsequently model their own propaganda apparatus. Convinced of propaganda's essential role in any political movement set on obtaining power, Hitler saw it as a vehicle of political salesmanship in a mass market.

The task of propaganda, Hitler argued, was to bring certain subjects to the attention of the masses. Propaganda should be simple, concentrating on a few essentials, which then had to be repeated many times, with emphasis on such emotional elements as love and hatred. Through the sustained uniformity of its application, propaganda, Hitler concluded, would lead to results "that are almost beyond our understanding." The Nazis did not make a distinction in their terminology between agitation and propaganda, unlike the Bolsheviks. In Soviet Russia, agitation was concerned with influencing the masses through ideas and slogans, while propaganda served to spread the ideology of Marxist-Leninism. The distinction dates back to Marxist theorist Georgi Plekhanov's famous definition, written in 1892: "A propagandist presents many ideas to one or a few persons; an agitator presents only one or a few ideas, but presents them to a whole mass of people." The Nazis, on the other hand, did not regard propaganda as merely an instrument for reaching the party elite, but rather as a means for the persuasion and indoctrination of all Germans.

World War II

The legacy of World War I was very important because it would largely determine how the belligerents viewed propaganda at the outbreak of hostilities in 1939. Thus, for all the negative connotations that have been attached to it, most governments were alert to the desirability in "total war" of utilizing propaganda to present their case to public both at home and abroad. In modern warfare, propaganda is required to (1) mobilize hatred against the enemy; (2) convince the population of the justness of one's own cause; (3) enlist the active support and cooperation of neutral countries; and (4) strengthen the support of one's allies. Having sought to pin war guilt on the enemy, the next step is to make the enemy appear savage, barbaric, and inhumane.

Philip M. Taylor has observed that "the Second World War witnessed the greatest propaganda battle in the history of warfare."[3] For six years, the belligerent states employed propaganda on a scale that dwarfed that of all other conflicts, including World War I. World War II was a battle between two new types of regime struggling for supremacy with one another in a battle for the future. Modern democracy and totalitarian dictatorship had both emerged from World War I and the outbreak of hostilities in 1939 was a testimony to their mutual incompatibility. There followed a struggle between mass societies, a war of political ideologies in which propaganda was a significant weapon.

Great Britain: "A People's War"

During World War II, authorities appropriated and controlled all forms of communication by means of strict censorship in order to requisition them for propaganda process. In the totalitarian states such as Italy, Germany, Japan, and the Soviet Union, this posed few problems, as the media—indeed the arts in general—had become part of the apparatus of the state. In liberal democracies, on the other hand, the effort proved more problematic. Nevertheless, on the propaganda front, Britain appeared to be better prepared than in World War I. A new MOI came into being within a matter of days after the declaration of war in 1939. But when set up, it was, to some extent, making up for lost ground. Morale would obviously be a crucial factor in enduring civilian bombing or a war of attrition, and the MOI would have to compete with totalitarian propaganda machines (of both Right and Left) that already were in existence for several years. The new ministry lacked authority in Whitehall and suffered from a difficult relationship with the press, which accused it of censoring and withholding news, and more generally of bureaucratic muddle. Nor, when it was first established, had the MOI any means of investigating or monitoring public opinion.

Interestingly, the MOI commissioned the psychologist, Professor Frederic Bartlett of Cambridge University, to write a monograph titled "Political Propaganda" in order to inform its thinking on mass psychology and propaganda. Bartlett's ideas, published in 1940, came to inform the ministry's thinking about the role that propaganda should play in a democracy engaged in "total war":

What is democracy? To this question all kinds of answers can be given. From the present point of view, however, one consideration overrides all others. In the modern world, political propaganda may be said to have been adopted as a weapon of State, but very nearly everywhere it has been adopted as the tool of a single political party within the State. This is precisely what can happen, except in a very incomplete way in a democratic country. A democracy differs from every other form of government in that it must always contain at least two main political parties, each treating the other with a very considerable degree of respect. Although each party may develop its own political propaganda, neither can violently suppress that of the other without destroying the spirit of democracy itself.[4]

In Fascist Italy, National Socialist Germany, or the Soviet Union, propaganda was to be controlled by the one party state, but in Britain, it was soon realized that if the MOI was to command the respect of the public then it should not be seen as an exclusive instrument of a single political party. The first minister of information, Lord Macmillan, was a Tory peer prompting the Labour leader, Clement Atlee to remark that he "was not satisfied that the Ministry of Information was not part of the Conservative machine."[5] Following the formation of Winston Churchill's coalition government in May 1940, the perceived bias within the MOI was remedied.

The MOI handled propaganda intended for home, Allied and neutral territory, and the Political Warfare Executive (PWE) dealt with enemy territory. The programs of the BBC earned Britain a powerful reputation for credibility that proved an asset long after the war ended. When Sir John Reith, the former director general of the BBC, was appointed minister for information in 1940, he laid down his two fundamental axioms: first, "news is the shock troops of propaganda"; second, that propaganda should tell "the truth, nothing but the truth and, as near as possible, the whole truth." George Orwell later observed: "The BBC as far as its news goes has gained enormous prestige since about 1940 . . . 'I heard it on the radio' is now almost equivalent to 'I know it must be true'."[6]

The incorporation of the censorship machinery of the Press and Censorship Bureau into the MOI in April 1940 (in contrast to the mistakes of World War I, when they remained separated) was an important organizational reform that reflected recognition of the need to integrate the control of news with the dissemination of positive propaganda. These principles were implemented so successfully that, according to Nicholas Pronay, "the press, the BBC and other organs of 'news' managed to maintain the trust of the British public at home and gained a reputation for Britain abroad for having even in wartime an honest, free and truthful media, yet which gave practically nothing of significance away to an ever-vigilant enemy."[7] By 1941, the system was operating so effectively that most observers were unaware that a sophisticated form of pre-censorship was in force, even within the BBC. This explains why Britain's wartime propaganda gained its reputation for telling the truth when, in fact, the whole truth could not be told.

In Britain, partly as a result of perceptions shaped by official propaganda, World War II was turning into a "people's war," and as Winston Churchill, prophesied to the House of Common in May 1901: "The wars of peoples will be more terrible than those of kings."[8]

Nazi Germany: The "Big Lie"

By contrast to John Reith's axioms that underpinned British propaganda, Hitler, as we have seen, believed implicitly in the concept of the "big lie"; but Reith had an unlikely fellow-traveler in the shape of Joseph Goebbels and his view that propaganda should be as accurate as possible. In Germany, a state propaganda machinery existed during peacetime, whereas in Britain it did not. The Reich Ministry for Popular Enlightenment and Propaganda (*Reichsministerium für Volksaufklärung und Propaganda*) under Goebbels was established shortly after the Nazis came to power in March 1933, meaning that when war broke out the Germans were already up and running with their propaganda activities.

The exigencies of war now demanded of Goebbels a more intense concern with the tactics of propaganda and greater flexibility to respond to changing military situations. His directive titled "Guidelines for the Execution of NSDAP [Nazi] Propaganda," issued at the outbreak of war, outlined the means he expected his staff to employ, which included the use of radio and newspapers, films, posters, mass meetings, illustrated lectures, and "whisper" or word-of-mouth propaganda (*Mundpropaganda*). During the course of the war, the changing military fortunes dictated four major German propaganda campaigns—on the themes of the *Blitzkrieg*, the campaign against the Soviet Union, total war and the need for strengthening morale, and promises of retaliation or revenge (*Vergeltung*).

From 1942 onward, Nazi propagandists were forced to shift their focus away from the initial euphoria of the *Blitzkrieg* victories to account for a rapidly deteriorating military situation. The impact of the Nazi defeat at Stalingrad on the morale of the German people cannot be over-estimated: it affected their attitude toward the war and created a crisis of confidence in the regime among broad sections of the population. Goebbels adopted a stance of frankness and realism by proclaiming "total war," demanding the complete mobilization of Germany's human resources for the war effort and attempting to elicit a fanaticism to fight to the death against Bolshevism. During the period 1943–1945, Nazi propaganda encouraged the population to believe that Germany was developing secret weapons capable of transforming the military situation. In these final years of the war, the notion of retaliation or revenge by means of these "miracle" weapons played a crucial role in sustaining morale and was widely seen as a panacea for all of Germany's troubles. However, dejection set in once it became apparent that the new weapons could not fulfil this promise.

In the final year of the war, Goebbels attempted to resurrect the Führer cult by depicting Hitler as a latter-day version of the 18th-century Prussian hero Frederick the Great, ultimately triumphant in the face of adversity. In the face of the gathering Russian occupation of Germany, this absurd image represented an alarming flight from reality that in March 1933.

In the face of the gathering Russian occupation of Germany, this absurd image represented an alarming flight from reality that no amount of propaganda could sustain. The "Hitler myth" could not survive the military reverses and was on the verge of extinction—along with the Third Reich.

The Soviet Union: "The Great Patriotic War"

Propaganda played a central role in the Soviet "Great Patriotic War," rallying the population to resist the Nazi invasion. The German attack (Operation

Barbarossa), trampling over the cynical 1939 Nazi-Soviet Nonaggression Pact, found Stalin's regime ill-prepared for battle. By the end of 1941, however, the German forces had lost their momentum. German military movements were increasingly hampered by harsh winter conditions, counter-attacks by partisans, and difficulties in maintaining overextended supply lines. At the same time, the Red Army had recovered from the initial setbacks and began to hit back.

After the initial shock, the formidable Soviet propaganda machine hit its stride quickly. Soviet propaganda was supervised by the Directorate of Propaganda and Agitation of the Central Committee under A. S. Shcherbakov and administered by the newly established Soviet Information Bureau. Within two days of the invasion, Commissar for Foreign Affairs Vyacheslav Molotov addressed the nation by radio in defiant tone. Newsreels captured the grim-faced determination of Soviet citizens while listening to his speech, images that were on Soviet cinema screens within a week. And one famous poster reminded the Soviet people: "Higher vigilance in every unit—always remember the treachery and baseness of the enemy!" Stalin was able to launch his call to arms at the start of July. He addressed his audience as "brothers and sisters" (eschewing the communist orthodoxy of "comrades") and called for a defense of the motherland (*rodina*).

In the spring of 1942, the German army renewed its offensive with the ultimate aim of crushing the city of Stalingrad. Soviet forces resisted heroically even after the Germans had reduced the city to rubble. The support of the Soviet people was crucial and in order to increase popular enthusiasm for the war, Stalin reshaped his domestic policies and official propaganda to heighten the patriotic spirit. As a result, nationalistic slogans replaced much of the Communist rhetoric in official pronouncements and the Soviet mass media. Propaganda celebrated the Russian army and people—soldiers and civilians—who bear expressions of grim determination or patriotic joy. The surrender of the German commander Friedrich von Paulus to the Soviet forces in January 1943 marked a decisive turning point in Soviet wartime propaganda which now presented the Soviet people united in an ideological struggle for a no-compromise victory. German soldiers and their leaders (notably Hitler and Goebbels) were depicted not only as brutal criminals out to ravage Russia and destroy communism, but Soviet propaganda exhibited the confidence to ridicule them as well.

United States: "Why We Fight"

The story of U.S. propaganda during World War II can be divided into two phases. During the period of neutrality, from September 1939 to December 1941, debate about the war raged among the population at large. The widespread feeling that the U.S. involvement in World War I had been a mistake cooled American reactions to the outbreak of war. The great neutrality debate began in earnest following the fall of France in June 1940. The pro-Allies lobby consisted of the moderate Committee to Defend America by Aiding the Allies and an actively interventionist Century Group (later known as the Fight for Freedom Committee). The pro-neutrality position was represented by the America First Committee. The isolationist camp included newspapers—especially those owned by William Randolph Hearst, the influential *Chicago Tribune*, and such well-known individuals as Charles Lindbergh. Both sides used rallies, petitions, and demonstrations to advance their causes. In Hollywood, Warner Bros. released a number of films with a political message, including *Foreign Correspondent* (1940) and *Confessions of a Nazi Spy* (1939). Isolationists in the Senate denounced such ventures as propaganda on behalf of Jewish and pro-British vested interests.

President Roosevelt initially took a backseat in the debate, but following his presidential election victory in 1940, he eventually pressured Britain to specify its war aims, which it was slow in doing. But the result, finally, was the Atlantic Charter of August 1941, which prepared the way for the postwar United Nations. The charter played its part in convincing the American people that the war was a noble cause and not just a bid to save the British Empire.

Once in the war, the U.S. government mobilized a major propaganda effort through the Office of War Information (OWI) and the Office of Strategic Services (OSS), the first having responsibility for overt or "white" propaganda, the second for covert or "black" propaganda. By 1945, the OWI had a staff of 130,000 and a budget of $110 million per year. The United States used propaganda to orient troops (most famously in the US Army Signal Corps film series *Why We Fight*, directed by Frank Capra) and to motivate its civilian population. In all phases of war propaganda, the commercial media played a key role (particularly Hollywood and the use of the commercial film industry). At home, campaigns conceived in collaboration with the commercial media included an effort to engage women in heavy-duty war work. During this campaign, *Saturday Evening Post* artist Norman Rockwell created the character of *Rosie the Riveter* whose iconic image become the personification of the emancipated American working woman in wartime.

Japan: "Thought War"

Japanese propaganda operated on three main fronts: domestically, China and Southeast Asia, and the West. Following its attack on the U.S. naval base at Pearl Harbor in December 1941, Japan had to fight on two fronts simultaneously—in China and the Pacific. The government disseminated propaganda claiming that it was Japan's manifest destiny to expand into Asia and bring Asia itself into the modern era.

Japanese propaganda, or the "Thought War" as they preferred to call it, was carried out by a variety of organizations. A "Bureau of Thought Supervision" based in the Ministry of Education had been in existence since 1932, but the Cabinet Information Bureau was not established until December 6, 1940, and was responsible for guiding the activities of the Japanese mass media. It consisted of 5 divisions and 17 sections, 550 officials in all. The division and section chiefs were selected from each government ministry, and the officials of each section were chosen from among civil public organizations (newspapers, motion pictures, book, and magazine companies).[9] Aside from the Cabinet Information Bureau, the Information Departments of the Army and Navy had primary responsibility for strategic information including the planning and execution of military propaganda.

Throughout the war, the Japanese made effective use of two major tools of mass media, cinema, and radio to support national morale and provide essential information for its home population. Both radio and film were rigorously controlled by the Japanese authorities and strict censorship controls prevented the portrayal of images or messages that might have a critical or detrimental effect upon the regime or its emperor.

Although the Cabinet Board of Information (loosely based on the Nazi's Ministry of Propaganda) officially managed nonmilitary propaganda, the Japanese employed a variety of institutions to assist with its propaganda campaigns. Privately owned entertainment companies such as film giants Toho and Shochiku and the entertainment company Yoshimoto sent platoons of entertainers to China to amuse the imperial troops. These brigades then returned to the home islands and publicized Japanese military success in China. Government-sponsored programs urged writers to reorganize into "voluntary" blocs and write about the effort to educate the civilian population during wartime. Semi-private advertising companies, employed as subcontractors for the Imperial General Headquarters, designed and produced propaganda leaflets that blanketed villages and fields in China and Southeast Asia. The Japanese military itself often distributed these materials and kept records of how local areas responded.

Official Japanese propaganda asked its people, already under duress since the 1930s, now to endure further economic restrictions, recycle scarce materials, make do with less, and live by slogans such as "luxury is the enemy." On the home front, the police and their various special agencies maintained careful surveillance of the domestic population, tabulating rumor campaigns, arresting so-called spies, and censoring media deemed anti-imperial. Intense propaganda campaigns directed at Japanese soldiers encouraged suicide over capture.[10]

The Home Front

In 1939–1945, civilians were in the frontline as never before. Advances in the technology of war, particularly in aerial bombing, served to transform their experience of war. Other advances meant that radio and cinema were now firmly established as mass media, and governments of all the belligerent states were conscious of the need to gauge the impact of propaganda. During the war, "feedback" agencies assessed the state of public opinion and the factors affecting public morale. In Britain, for example, this involved using the results of the Home Intelligence Reports and the social-research Mass Observation project, while in Germany the weekly reports of the SS Security Service (*Sicherheitsdienst der SS*) made it their business to gauge the mood and morale of the people. In the United States, pollsters employed sampling methods both for commercial polls—such as those conducted by Roper and Gallup—and public-interest polls, such as those generated by the Office of Public Opinion Research (OPOR) and the National Opinion Research Center (NORC).

All the belligerents reinforced the central message of World War I—the importance of citizens contributing to the war effort. In Britain, the theme of "your country needs you" manifested itself in the notion of a shared "people's war"—a nation working together (as in the slogan "Let Us Go Forward Together") and putting aside class, regional, and social differences. This strategy was also applied across the British Empire. As the public wanted to be reassured of the nation's capacity to produce armaments and their effective use, artistic compositions of industrial sites and workers produced a new iconography. Office and factories were stages for a shifting social order, adjusted and attuned to wartime needs. Propaganda also stressed the new roles undertaken by women for the war effort—from performing menial tasks with the Auxiliary Territorial Service to complex work in armaments factories. Bearing in mind the unmet promises (the land "fit for heroes") made during World War I, British propaganda also emphasized the possibility of postwar change—which, in the end, paved the way for the Labour election victory in 1945.

In the United States, because of acute wartime labor shortages, women were needed in the defense industries, the civil service and the armed forces. Despite the continuing trend for women to enter the work force, propaganda campaigns targeted those women who had never before held jobs. The images that were produced glorified and glamorized the roles of working women and suggested that a woman's femininity need not be compromised by work. Typists, for example, were recruited with such slogans as "Victory Waits on Your Fingers—Keep 'Em Flying, Miss U.S.A." Whether fulfilling their duty in the home, factory, office or military, women were invariably presented as attractive, confident, and resolved to do their part to win the war. The *Saturday Evening Post* artist Norman Rockwell created the character of Rosie the Riveter, a variation of this stereotype, who became the personification of the emancipated American woman in wartime. Rosie had big muscular arms and put her penny loafers on top of a copy of Hitler's *Mein Kampf*.

Rockwell also disseminated President Roosevelt's Four Freedoms, which appealed to the nation's resolve by setting out America's freedom of speech and worship, and freedom from fear and from want. In conjunction with the OWI, he produced a series of posters illustrating each of these freedoms in a highly successful war-bond drive.

By the outbreak of war, film had become *the* mass medium. In wartime, going to the cinema remained what it had become in the 1930s, a normal part of everyday life, by far the most popular form of entertainment, particularly for the working class. It was, unsurprisingly, exploited extensively for propaganda purposes by all the belligerent countries. In Britain, where, by the end of the war, 30 million people were going to the cinema every week, the MOI commissioned morale-boosting films, including documentaries exemplifying British courage or military prowess: *Desert Victory* (1943), about the defeat of Rommel at El Alamein; Humphrey Jennings's exceptional body of work, including *London Can Take It* (1940), about the unfolding German bombing campaign of the "Blitz"; and Harry Watts's *Target for Tonight* (1941), about an RAF bombing raid on Germany. The commercial film industry, in conjunction with the MOI, portrayed many of the personal experiences of the war. The task was to reconcile individual needs and experience with the necessity of pulling together and to bring out the defining qualities of Britishness such as stoicism and understatement, the "stiff-upper lip" and the sense of fair play. The result was a series of films about people from different backgrounds and classes successfully welded together for the fight against Nazism, such as *In Which We Serve* (1942), *Millions Like Us* (1943), *The Way Ahead* (1944), and Jennings's *Fires Were Started* (1943).

In Germany, where the cinema was equally popular and wartime cinema audiences were increasing, Goebbels's strategy (*Filmpolitik*) shrewdly mixed entertainment with propaganda. Documentaries—most famously, Leni Reifenstahl's *Triumph of the Will* (1935)—and the newsreels (*Deutsche Wochenschauen*) provided overt propaganda of Nazi ideology and German military successes, whereas feature films were expected to reflect the ambience of National Socialism rather than loudly proclaiming its ideology. *Soldiers of Tomorrow* (*Soldaten von Morgen*, 1941) took a humorous swipe at the British public-school system and the resultant degeneracy of British youth, comparing it unfavorably with the Hitler Youth. More generally, feature films were musicals or love stories with a Nazi twist.

The United States used official propaganda to orient troops and to motivate its civilian population, most famously in the U.S. Army Signal Corps film series *Why We Fight* directed by Frank Capra. Hollywood, however, was quick to mobilize and enlist in the war cause. Many of the films produced during the war were patriotic rallying cries that affirmed a sense of national purpose. Combat films of the war years emphasized patriotism, group effort, and the value of individual sacrifices for a larger cause. Films like *Flying Tigers* (1942), *Wake Island* (1942), *Air Force* (1943), *Destination Tokyo* (1943), *Guadalcanal Diary* (1943), *Thirty Seconds over Tokyo* (1944), and *Objective, Burma!* (1945) gave viewers on the home front a vicarious sense of participating in the war.

While each major belligerent demonstrated, in films and the other media, its own propaganda strategy for its own population, common traits did emerge. Propagandists, whether Allied or Axis, exhorted their citizens to produce more, to eat less, to conserve scarce resources, to keep their lips sealed—and, of course, to keep hating the enemy.

World War II witnessed a vast proliferation of media production, from state-sponsored posters, pamphlets, radio, and films (including newsreels) to commercial newspapers, comics, and military newspapers. The Soviet Union boasted no less than 757 military titles by 1945, and as for radio, the BBC increased its foreign-language services from 10 in 1939 to 45 by 1943. The U.S. government inaugurated the multilingual Voice of America network in 1942, for external broadcasting, while at home the amount of radio airtime devoted to news rose from 5 percent to 20 percent—with 9 out of 10 Americans listening to 4 hours of radio daily. Toward the end of the war, the Nazi government was also trialing television for a limited German audience.[11]

The sources that are included in this volume are intended to reflect this proliferation and represent as wide a range of propaganda artifacts as possible. This book is intended to be the definitive text on political propaganda in World War II. It will analyze propaganda, its history, theory, and practice by means of documentary source material—both visual and written, official and unofficial. It will look at all forms of propaganda, "white," "black," and "grey" and how such propaganda was disseminated in changing military contexts during the conflict. The distinctive feature of the book will be the manner in which the content, style, and significance of the sources is analyzed. The commentary and the sources are not discrete, rather merge to become of a continuous and integrated narrative. Films, posters, leaflets, paintings, pamphlets, newspapers, cartoons, radio, coins, stamps, and monuments,—propaganda has access to ever more complex and versatile media in its many-faceted attempts to boost the morale of one side and undermine the will of the other. All will be discussed in this wide-ranging analysis.

Notes

1. For a wider discussion of the roots and antecedents of the term "propaganda," including shifting historical definitions see, D. Welch, *Propaganda, Power and Persuasion* (London: British Library/Chicago: Chicago University Press, 2013), 1–40.

2. In-depth analyses of propaganda during World War I can be found in M. Saunders and P. M. Taylor, *British Propaganda during the First World War, 1914–18* (London: Macmillan, 1982); G. S. Messinger, *British Propaganda and the State in the First World War* (Manchester: Manchester University Press, 1992); D. Welch, *Germany, Propaganda and Total War, 1914–1918. The Sins of Omission* (New Brunswick: Rutgers University Press, 2000, revised edition); *Germany and Propaganda in World War I: Pacifism, Mobilization and Total War* (London: I.B. Tauris, 2014).

3. P. M. Taylor, *Munitions of the Mind: A History of Propaganda from the Ancient World to the Present Day* (Manchester: Manchester University Press, 1995), 210.

4. F. Bartlett, *Political Propaganda* (Cambridge: Cambridge University Press, 1940), 16.

5. Cited by Sir John Reith in his memoir, *Into the Wind* (London: Hodder & Stoughton, 1949).

6. Quoted in P. Lashmar and J. Oliver, *Britain's Secret Propaganda War* (Stroud: Sutton, 1998), 19.

7. N. Pronay, "The News and the Media," in N. Pronay and D. W. Spring (eds.), *Propaganda, Politics and Film, 1918–45* (London: Macmillan, 1982), 174.

8. Quoted in P. Addison, *Churchill on the Home Front 1900–1955* (London: Jonathan Cape, 1992), 19.

9. Information taken from Namikawa Ryo, "Japanese Overseas Broadcasting: A Personal View," in K.R.M. Short (ed.), *Film and Radio Propaganda in World War II* (London: Croom Helm, 1983), 321. Namikawa was a member of the Cabinet Information Bureau during World War II.

10. See, B. Kushner's entry "Japan in World War II" in N. Cull, D. Culbert, and D. Welch, *Propaganda and Mass Persuasion. A Historical Encyclopedia, 1500 to the Present* (Santa Barbara, CA: ABC-CLIO, 2003), 444–445.

11. See, D. Welch, *Propaganda: Power and Persuasion*, 20.

Chapter 1
The Propaganda War

Document 1

BASIC GROUND RULES OF BRITISH PROPAGANDA DURING WORLD WAR II (JUNE 21, 1939)

Document

Secret

International Propaganda and Broadcasting Enquiry

Propaganda Notions (Various Sources)

I. *General Ideas for Propaganda*

1. In a stratified society persuade the dominant group.

2. To convince the educated minority, propaganda must be subtle and indirect (Mark Antony's speech is a perfect example of cautious propaganda) on the feeling-its-way principle. (Hitler's method is the opposite.)

3. As regards the masses of people, appeal to their instincts and not to their reason.

4. Propaganda should fit the pre-conceived impressions, e.g., a Chinaman thinks every foreigner a cunning person who is prepared to use a concealed gun should wiliness 'fail.

5. In propaganda we should concentrate on a definite object to fit pre-conceived ideas.

6. Evils against which propaganda is directed should, if possible, be personified (e.g., the scarification by the German Press of President Benes).

7. Essentials of propaganda method are as follows:

    (i) *Repetition* (and from Topical angles).

    (ii) *Colour* (obstructions to be avoided in favour of personalities).

    (iii) *A measure of the truth*, or at any rate keeping the lie just in front of the ultimate revelation (the case of the Sudenten Germans).

    (iv) *Building round a slogan* ("that scrap of paper")

    (v) *Propaganda* should be directed towards a specific objective (pick out key people and study them hard). Then proceed to groups, e.g., during the War the German concentrated on persuading the U.S.A. Congress to stop sales of munitions to all combatants. Similarly, allied propaganda might exploit the minorities in Germany and racial groups abroad.

8. *The motive should be concealed.* This does not exclude overlapping with open propaganda. Thus the doctored speeches of foreign statesmen reproduced in Germany are a contemporary example of such overlapping. (Again patriotic societies abroad subsidized by all armament firms have been found to launch campaigns for bigger defence forces. Again, war scares send up armament shares.)

9. *Timing.* For example, Lloyd George's Saturday afternoon speeches provided hot news for the evening papers, secured full Sunday publicity, and an extra lot on the Monday. Again, propaganda concerning luxury goods would, for example, concentrate on places where trade is booming; whilst it is a well-known practice to hold up bad news until it can be counter-balanced by good news.

   One of the best declarations of successful timing was the British declaration during the late war making cotton unconditional contraband. This regulation was issued just when the U.S.A. press was full of the sinking of the 'Arabic,' and had no time for more important matters.

10. The general sequence of propaganda is:
    (i)   Do the ground-work;
    (ii) Then the mass attack;
    (iii) Clear up the remainder.

11. Radio can be isolated to minorities overseas but cannot pick out classes in this country.

12. Films are similarly handicapped.

13. In propaganda a judicious reticence is as important as positive emphasis.

14. One of the aims of propaganda is to awaken the social conscience. For this purpose the assistance of the psychologist cannot be ignored.

15. According to Hitler, propaganda should use basic ideas and should address itself solely to the masses.

16. One should give clarity and precision to half-formed and nebulous ideas that are shaping the public mind. The introduction of fresh ideas is harder.

17. The possibility of steamships must not be neglected.

18. The best propaganda is the silent murder of the opposition news—Censorship.

19. Under censorship conditions rumour assumes gigantic proportions. Hence whispering campaigns.

20. Trappings and pageantry inherited from the past form valuable propaganda for stability.

21. 43% of film-goers in U.K. pay no more than 7d. Another 37% pay not more than 1/-. Hence the cinema provides the great mass-audience.

22. "No matter how innocent and free from controversy a story may appear, a film producer must handle it with kid gloves and walk on eggs until it is completed."

23. The film cannot be effectively contradicted.

24. Weather reports must be censored.

25. Retaliatory propaganda in peace-time may provoke war by departing from the democracies' principle that every state has the right to organize its own life as it thinks fit without meddling elsewhere.

26. The propaganda of the democracies must demonstrate that war would be fatal to the dictators.

27. We must get hold of all the big financial houses everywhere.

28. A particularly effective means of propaganda is the idealization of national heroes.

29. Even scientific publications may serve propaganda purpose by being judiciously distributed in isolated numbers. They keep the name afloat.

30. A useful device is to get a neutral to state our national case.

31. The glorification of the Royal Family is an important publicity matter.

32. The ideal function of propaganda is to win popular support for a cause by captivating the emotions *and* flattering the reason of the public (i.e. Men like to *think* that they are acting according to reason even if in reality emotion and other non-rational forces are, as so often, much stronger determinants). Popular propaganda should substitute emotion for reason under the guise of facilitating the process of reasoning.

33. Propaganda is a machine for generating and maintaining enthusiasm. Propaganda should therefore:

    (i) Never be dull.

    (ii) Never be offensive to its audience.

34. The highest art in propaganda is to maintain the appearance of impartiality, while securing the wholehearted adoption of the view propagated.

35. As regards fundamentals many people are vainer and idler than they imagine or admit. Propaganda should take notice of this.

36. "The marching-tune sets the blood coursing faster than do the battle-standards." This maxim should probably be borne in mind despite the fact that the English are not a remarkably musical people.

37. Propaganda measures in time of war should always be tested by the simple question, "Will this measure increase people's desire to serve

and to keep on serving?" Exceptions may occasionally occur owing to overriding considerations of Foreign Policy, but this should not affect the general rule.

38. The English public likes competitions (e.g. football pools and cross-word puzzles). Propaganda should take note of this.

39. Intellectual reasoning should be as objective as possible. Propaganda is, in its very nature, subjective. It is subjective because:

    (i) A specific object (e.g. national victory in a war) should inform all its arguments, methods of presentation, etc.

    (ii) Propaganda should appeal largely to non-rational elements which are more susceptible to subjective than to objective influence (e.g. Issues should be presented in personalized form as far as possible). The subjective approach usually has greater dramatic appeal than the objective.

II. *Suggestions for Foreign Propaganda*

    1. As regards Dominions and Colonies, get hold of the big people here having relations and friends over there.

    2. In the East the question of prestige is all important.

    3. As regards the Germans, their national inferiority complex is a basic factor in propaganda among them.

    4. South America is served by A.P. and Havas of France. England is largely excluded.

    5. In the German Propaganda Memorandum on Spain (1935) it is said that it is better to influence smaller rather than the larger Spanish news agencies. Larger ones would demand more money and would not be such unquestioning allies. There is nothing more effective than a good news agency for influencing public opinion. "It is, so to speak, the skeleton, while commenting and reporting are the flesh. Only the two together can make a live body capable of doing the work."

    6. South America. The most southerly States of Brazil—Santa Catherina and Rio Grande do Sul—contain large colonies of Germans who for many years have been taught to consider Germany as their Fatherland, and not Brazil. There are said to be 2,000,000 Germans in Brazil.

    7. It may be possible to feed anti-British newspapers with French news.

    8. The Italian colonies in the United States, South America (especially Brazil and Argentine) and Australia are kept in close contact with the homeland. It might be noted that the Argentine quickly absorbs Italians and turns them into staunch Argentinians.

9. In Australia the Italian colony has been the means of promoting hostility towards Italy and Fascism.

10. The Italian atrocities in Libya give us a useful point. (The ruthless nature of Marshal Graziani's conquest.)

11. From the outset Hitler concentrated on colour, symbolism and spectacular displays. (The German thinks in images.)

12. The 25 unalterable points of the Nazi programme (stated to be fixed for all time) should form in increasing measure points d'appui for our propaganda against them.

13. Rotarians are banned in Germany: so also is the P.E.N. Club.

14. The only countries where there is a genuinely free press are the British Empire (excluding India and Palestine), U.S., Holland, Switzerland and perhaps Scandinavia.

15. In Argentine provincial journals were offered by Italian and German bureau free telegraphic news. Subsidies to newspapers in the Argentine as well as in some of the smaller states have been reported.

16. China banned the British film "Jack Ahoy" because the story of naval life included a burlesque of Chinese pirates.

17. Japan rejected the film "The King Steps Out" because it tended to ridicule royalty.

18. Russia leads with community listening-in.

19. Our German propaganda should emphasise the essential conditions under which German friendship can endure.

20. In America the British position about war debts needs repeated exposition.

21. The German war literature must be searched to provide propaganda points.

22. An International paper in Esperanto would probably be necessary.

23. The publication of lists of German prisoners in our publications will tend to make them read by German colonies abroad.

24. We must also produce a magazine for prisoners of war in this country containing such information.

25. We must search Hitler's speeches for propaganda points.

26. We must search allied and neutral literature for anti-German material—especially Spanish literature.

III. *Past Experience in Propaganda*

1. The German propaganda before Caporetto included the lavish distribution by secret agents of faked Italian newspapers among the troops.

2. As showing the importance of counter-espionage, the deciphering of a Nauen radio message by the Admiralty, proposing an alliance between Germany, Mexico, and Japan, gave the coup-de-grace to German propaganda in the U.S.A.

3. The time factor is vital. Thus the Zinoviev letter—which was the same as scores of others from Moscow—was exposed at just the right moment, when the public were mistrustful of Russia and began to dislike the British Labour Party.

4. Japan distributed free wireless sets in Manchuria.

5. Italy gives young Arabs a free holiday in Italy.

6. The Germans have a special section in propaganda machine to counteract atrocity propaganda, to win over foreign journalists, and to watch the foreign press, so that papers containing undesirable matter may be confiscated on their arrival in Germany.

7. Italy and Germany believe in mass visits. Thus in January, 1918, 1,500 Roumanians went to Rome at the expense of the Italian Government. Similarly, thousands of Italian children abroad are taken to Italy annually for a holiday.

8. Mussolini's habit of personal reception is invaluable propaganda: he impresses and flatters.

9. The Italians have already employed travelling cinema vans in Palestine showing faked films of Jewish atrocities against the Arabs.

10. A special propaganda section of the Red Army was formed and 16 super planes planned for its use. The Maxim Gorki, built in 1933, had a wing spread of 630 feet: it could be heard from 4,000 feet for 200 miles. It also carried a printing plant which could turn out 4,000 leaflets an hour.

11. In Germany cinema attendances have risen despite the injection of more and more propaganda into the programme.

12. In 1934 there were more than 30,000 cinemas in Russia.

13. The foreign films used in Russia are carefully edited by a special Department.

14. During the Great War the U.S.A. Government Films were run at a profit. Overseas exhibitors who refused to show the U.S.A. Government films were boycotted; so too were those who used German films.

15. Poland cut out of "Show-boat" the lines in "Ole Man River":

     "You and me we sweat and strain

     Body all achin' and racked with pain"

     on the ground that they were likely to stir up class enmity.

16. "Italian cinemas in the near East, e.g. add to the respect for Fascism by showing pictures of Italian military might, in contrast with some very dull and staid news items from Britain."

17. During the last War the Germans ran a comic paper printed in Spanish (we ran one in Russia).

18. One of the German failures last time was the use of statistics in amorphous and detrimental masses.

19. Experience has tended to prove that in public meetings addressed to local audiences a speaker carries more weight through local reputation than through national eminence.

20. It is reported from one source that during the Great War it was found that one good poster would do the work of about twenty public meetings.

21. In *Mein Kampf* it is stated that the colour combination which produces the greatest psychological reaction is red, black, and white. (Hence the German national colours.)

Source: U.K. National Archives, INF 1/724. Contains public sector information licensed under the Open Government Licence v3.0.

Analysis

The document can be found in the archives of Britain's second Ministry of Information (MOI) held at the Public Record Office in London. It is a memorandum, dated June 21, 1939, containing 86 basic ground rules that the Royal Institute of International Affairs, which commissioned the enquiry into Broadcasting and Propaganda, considered would be of value to the planners of the embryonic MOI.

Compared with the outbreak of World War I, Britain appeared to be better prepared in 1939. The second MOI had been planned for some time and came into being within a matter of days after Britain declared war on Germany. However, appearances were deceptive. Planning for the conduct of propaganda can be traced back to October 1935 when a subcommittee of the Committee of Imperial Defence (CID), chaired by John Colville, was appointed to draw up secret guidelines for a new ministry in the event of war. In 1936, following the committee's recommendations, Sir Stephen Tallents, a civil servant who had been head of the Empire Marketing Board, was appointed as MOI director-general designate. When the MOI was partially mobilized on September 26, 1938, it did so amidst chaos and confusion. Tallents's problem was trying to make any kind of headway. Of the small group of Whitehall officials who knew of its existence, few were confident of the ministry's ability to combat effectively the already tried and tested machinery of the Nazi's Ministry of Propaganda if war did break out. Tallents was eventually viewed as a troublemaker and sacked in 1938 after the Munich crisis[1] when he began to push for greater clarity, and the Public Trustee, Sir Ernest Fass, was brought in. Fass had little idea of what he was doing. He lasted four months and then an equally inappropriate choice was made, the ageing former diplomat Lord Perth. Perth did not last long either and the next choice was Lord Macmillan, an elderly Scottish barrister, who was in post when the war broke out.

The Munich "dress rehearsal" provided the British planners with both time and opportunity to remedy the deficiencies exposed by the crisis. One of the most important lessons to be drawn was in the field of propaganda techniques. Before 1939, little attention had been devoted to various techniques of disseminating propaganda. British officials were far more preoccupied with constructing the appropriate structure and machinery. Using Lord Beaverbrook's model of 1918 as a blueprint for their new ministry, the planners, led by Sir Stephen Tallents, had recognized some of the essential truth of propaganda in wartime, namely the connection between propaganda and censorship. The biggest difficulty the MOI would have to face would be that of news management. How could a nation which prided itself on freedom of speech and information become an overbearing sensor, particularly if it chose to fight in the name of freedom? But they had too readily accepted that the methods employed during World War I, could equally be applied to a war against Fascism and Nazism. Moreover, the planners failed initially to recognize that advances in communication technology in areas such as broadcasting and the cinema had widened the possibilities offered by propaganda.

Although Britain entered World War II relatively ill-equipped to conduct effective propaganda, it made considerable progress during the final year of peace. As war became increasingly likely, the nucleus of the MOI was finally permitted to recruit the services of interested experts and outside organizations such as Chatham House.[2] This document reveals that a considerable degree was devoted to the question of propaganda methods and techniques, albeit rather late in the day. The ground rules set out here might appear somewhat fundamental, even naïve ("propaganda should fit the preconceived impressions, e.g., a Chinaman thinks every foreigner a cunning person who is prepared to use a concealed gun should wiliness fail"). But, interestingly, they reveal that those who drafted the secret document were familiar with Hitler's view on propaganda that he published in *Mein Kampf* (My Struggle). Not only that, but they appeared to endorse some Hitlerite propaganda principles. For example, point 3 of the document states, "As regards the masses of the people, appeal to their instincts and not to their reason," and point 7 refers to the importance of building on slogans and the need for repetition.

When World War II started, the British government decided not to take over the media or suppress editorial freedom but rather to allow debate and interpretation. However, it would control the flow of information to the media. In spite of a number of its eccentricities, this planning document formed the foundations of the basic principles of Britain's war time propaganda. When Sir John Reith was appointed Minister of Information in 1940, he laid down two of the ministry's fundamental axioms for the balance of the war: that news equated to the "shock troops of propaganda" and the view that it was more effective that propaganda should tell "the truth, nothing but the truth and, as near as possible, the whole truth."

Document 2

PRESIDENT ROOSEVELT'S "FOUR FREEDOMS" SPEECH (JANUARY 6, 1941)

Document

Mr. President, Mr. Speaker, Members of the Seventy-seventh Congress:

I address you, the Members of this new Congress, at a moment unprecedented in the history of the Union. I use the word "unprecedented," because at no previous time has American security been as seriously threatened from without as it is today. Since the permanent formation of our Government under the Constitution, in 1789, most of the periods of crisis in our history have related to our domestic affairs. And fortunately, only one of these—the four-year War Between the States—ever threatened our national unity. Today, thank God, one hundred and thirty million Americans, in forty-eight States, have forgotten points of the compass in our national unity.

It is true that prior to 1914 the United States often had been disturbed by events in other Continents. We had even engaged in two wars with European nations and in a number of undeclared wars in the West Indies, in the Mediterranean and in the Pacific for the maintenance of American rights and for the principles of peaceful commerce. But in no case had a serious threat been raised against our national safety or our continued independence.

What I seek to convey is the historic truth that the United States as a nation has at all times maintained opposition, clear, definite opposition, to any attempt to lock us in behind an ancient Chinese wall while the procession of civilization went past. Today, thinking of our children and of their children, we oppose enforced isolation for ourselves or for any other part of the Americas.

That determination of ours, extending over all these years, was proved, for example, in the early days during the quarter century of wars following the French Revolution. While the Napoleonic struggles did threaten interests of the United States because of the French foothold in the West Indies and in Louisiana, and while we engaged in the War of 1812 to vindicate our right to peaceful trade, it is nevertheless clear that neither France nor Great Britain, nor any other nation, was aiming at domination of the whole world.

And in like fashion from 1815 to 1914—ninety-nine years—no single war in Europe or in Asia constituted a real threat against our future or against the future of any other American nation. Except in the Maximilian interlude in Mexico, no foreign power sought to establish itself in this Hemisphere; and the strength of the British fleet in the Atlantic has been a friendly strength. It is still a friendly strength. Even when the World War broke out in 1914, it seemed to contain only small threat of danger to our own American future. But, as time went on, as we remember, the American people began to visualize what the downfall of democratic nations might mean to our own democracy.

We need not overemphasize imperfections in the Peace of Versailles. We need not harp on failure of the democracies to deal with problems of world reconstruction. We should remember that the Peace of 1919 was far less unjust than the kind of "pacification" which began even before Munich, and which is being carried on under the new order of tyranny that seeks to spread over every continent today. The American people have unalterably set their faces against that tyranny.

I suppose that every realist knows that the democratic way of life is at this moment being directly assailed in every part of the world—assailed either by arms, or by secret spreading of poisonous propaganda by those who seek to destroy unity and promote discord in nations that are still at peace. During six-teen long months this assault has blotted out the whole pattern of democratic life in an appalling number of independent nations, great and small. And the assailants are still on the march, threatening other nations, great and small.

Therefore, as your President, performing my constitutional duty to "give to the Congress information of the state of the Union," I find it, unhappily, necessary to report that the future and the safety of our country and of our democracy are overwhelmingly involved in events far beyond our borders.

Armed defense of democratic existence is now being gallantly waged in four continents. If that defense fails, all the population and all the resources of Europe, and Asia, and Africa and Australasia will be dominated by conquerors. And let us remember that the total of those populations in those four continents, the total of those populations and their resources greatly exceeds the sum total of the population and the resources of the whole of the Western Hemisphere—yes, many times over. In times like these it is immature—and incidentally, untrue—for anybody to brag that an unprepared America, single-handed, and with one hand tied behind its back, can hold off the whole world. No realistic American can expect from a dictator's peace international generosity, or return of true independence, or world disarmament, or freedom of expression, or freedom of religion—or even good business. Such a peace would bring no security for us or for our neighbors. "Those, who would give up essential liberty to purchase a little temporary safety, deserve neither liberty nor safety."

As a nation, we may take pride in the fact that we are softhearted; but we cannot afford to be soft-headed. We must always be wary of those who with sounding brass and a tinkling cymbal preach the "ism" of appeasement. We must especially beware of that small group of selfish men who would clip the wings of the American eagle in order to feather their own nests. I have recently pointed out how quickly the tempo of modern warfare could bring into our very midst the physical attack which we must eventually expect if the dictator nations win this war.

There is much loose talk of our immunity from immediate and direct invasion from across the seas. Obviously, as long as the British Navy retains its power, no such danger exists. Even if there were no British Navy, it is not probable that any enemy would be stupid enough to attack us by landing troops in the United States from across thousands of miles of ocean, until it had acquired strategic bases from which to operate. But we learn much from the lessons of the past years in Europe—particularly the lesson of Norway, whose essential seaports were captured by treachery and surprise built up over a series of years.

The first phase of the invasion of this Hemisphere would not be the landing of regular troops. The necessary strategic points would be occupied by secret agents and by their dupes—and great numbers of them are already here, and in Latin America. As long as the aggressor nations maintain the offensive, they—not we—will choose the time and the place and the method of their attack. And that is why the future of all the American Republics is today in serious danger. That is why this Annual Message to the Congress is unique in our history. That is why every member of the Executive Branch of the Government and every member of the Congress face great responsibility and great accountability.

The need of the moment is that our actions and our policy should be devoted primarily—almost exclusively—to meeting this foreign peril. For all our domestic problems are now a part of the great emergency. Just as our national policy in internal affairs has been based upon a decent respect for the rights and the dignity of all of our fellow men within our gates, so our national policy in foreign affairs has been based on a decent respect for the rights and the dignity of all nations, large and small. And the justice of morality must and will win in the end.

Our national policy is this: First, by an impressive expression of the public will and without regard to partisanship, we are committed to all-inclusive national defense. Second, by an impressive expression of the public will and without regard to partisanship, we are committed to full support of all those resolute people everywhere who are resisting aggression and are thereby keeping war away from our Hemisphere. By this support, we express our determination that the democratic cause shall prevail; and we strengthen the defense and the security of our own nation. Third, by an impressive expression of the public will and without regard to partisanship, we are committed to the proposition that principles of morality and considerations for our own security will never permit us to acquiesce in a peace dictated by aggressors and sponsored by appeasers. We know that enduring peace cannot be bought at the cost of other people's freedom.

In the recent national election there was no substantial difference between the two great parties in respect to that national policy. No issue was fought out on this line before the American electorate. And today it is abundantly evident that American citizens everywhere are demanding and supporting speedy and complete action in recognition of obvious danger.

Therefore, the immediate need is a swift and driving increase in our armament production. Leaders of industry and labor have responded to our summons. Goals of speed have been set. In some cases these goals are being reached ahead of time; in some cases we are on schedule; in other cases there are slight but not serious delays; and in some cases—and I am sorry to say very important cases—we are all concerned by the slowness of the accomplishment of our plans.

The Army and Navy, however, have made substantial progress during the past year. Actual experience is improving and speeding up our methods of production with every passing day. And today's best is not good enough for tomorrow. I am not satisfied with the progress thus far made. The men in charge of the program represent the best in training, in ability, and in patriotism. They are not satisfied with the progress thus far made. None of us will be satisfied until the job is done. No matter whether the original goal was set too high or too low, our objective is quicker and better results. We are behind schedule in turning out finished airplanes; we are working day and night to solve the innumerable problems and to catch up.

We are ahead of schedule in building warships but we are working to get even further ahead of that schedule. To change a whole nation from a basis of peacetime production of implements of peace to a basis of wartime production of implements of war is no small task. And the greatest difficulty comes at the beginning of the program, when new tools, new plant facilities, new assembly lines, and new ship ways must first be constructed before the actual materiel begins to flow steadily and speedily from them.

The Congress, of course, must rightly keep itself informed at all times of the progress of the program. However, there is certain information, as the Congress itself will readily recognize, which, in the interests of our own security and those of the nations that we are supporting, must of needs be kept in confidence. New circumstances are constantly begetting new needs for our safety. I shall ask this Congress for greatly increased new appropriations and authorizations to carry on what we have begun.

I also ask this Congress for authority and for funds sufficient to manufacture additional munitions and war supplies of many kinds, to be turned over to those nations which are now in actual war with aggressor nations. Our most useful and immediate role is to act as an arsenal for them as well as for ourselves. They do not need man power, but they do need billions of dollars worth of the weapons of defense. The time is near when they will not be able to pay for them all in ready cash. We cannot, and we will not, tell them that they must surrender, merely because of present inability to pay for the weapons which we know they must have.

I do not recommend that we make them a loan of dollars with which to pay for these weapons—a loan to be repaid in dollars.

I recommend that we make it possible for those nations to continue to obtain war materials in the United States, fitting their orders into our own program. And nearly all of their materiel would, if the time ever came, be useful in our own defense. Taking counsel of expert military and naval authorities, considering what is best for our own security, we are free to decide how much should be kept here and how much should be sent abroad to our friends who by their determined and heroic resistance are giving us time in which to make ready our own defense.

For what we send abroad, we shall be repaid, repaid within a reasonable time following the close of hostilities, repaid in similar materials, or, at our option, in other goods of many kinds, which they can produce and which we need. Let us say to the democracies: "We Americans are vitally concerned in your defense of freedom. We are putting forth our energies, our resources and our organizing powers to give you the strength to regain and maintain a free world. We shall send you, in ever-increasing numbers, ships, planes, tanks, guns. This is our purpose and our pledge."

In fulfillment of this purpose we will not be intimidated by the threats of dictators that they will regard as a breach of international law or as an act of war our aid to the democracies which dare to resist their aggression. Such aid . . . such aid is not an act of war, even if a dictator should unilaterally proclaim it so to be. And when the dictators, if the dictators, are ready to make war upon us, they will not wait for an act of war on our part. They did not wait for Norway or Belgium or the Netherlands to commit an act of war. Their only interest is in a new one-way international law, which lacks mutuality in its observance, and, therefore, becomes an instrument of oppression.

The happiness of future generations of Americans may well depend upon how effective and how immediate we can make our aid felt. No one can tell the exact character of the emergency situations that we may be called upon to meet. The Nation's hands must not be tied when the Nation's life is in danger. Yes, and we must all prepare—all of us prepare—to make the sacrifices that the emergency—almost as serious as war itself—demands. Whatever stands in the way of speed and efficiency in defense—in defense preparations of any kind—must give way to the national need. A free nation has the right to expect full cooperation from all groups. A free nation has the right to look to the leaders of business, of labor, and of agriculture to take the lead in stimulating effort, not among other groups but within their own groups.

The best way of dealing with the few slackers or trouble makers in our midst is, first, to shame them by patriotic example, and, if that fails, to use the sovereignty of government to save government. As men do not live by bread alone, they do not fight by armaments alone. Those who man our defenses, and those behind them who build our defenses, must have the stamina and the courage which come from unshakable belief in the manner of life which they are defending. The mighty action that we are calling for cannot be based on a disregard of all things worth fighting for.

The Nation takes great satisfaction and much strength from the things which have been done to make its people conscious of their individual stake in the preservation of democratic life in America. Those things have toughened the fibre of our people, have renewed their faith and strengthened their devotion to the institutions we make ready to protect. Certainly this is no time for any of us to stop thinking about the social and economic problems which are the root cause of the social revolution which is today a supreme factor in the world. For there is nothing mysterious about the foundations of a healthy and strong democracy. The basic things expected by our people of their political and economic systems are simple. They are:

Equality of opportunity for youth and for others.

Jobs for those who can work.

Security for those who need it.

The ending of special privilege for the few.

The preservation of civil liberties for all.

The enjoyment . . . the enjoyment of the fruits of scientific progress in a wider and constantly rising standard of living. These are the simple, the basic things that must never be lost sight of in the turmoil and unbelievable complexity of our modern world. The inner and abiding strength of our economic and political systems is dependent upon the degree to which they fulfill these expectations. Many subjects connected with our social economy call for immediate improvement. As examples:

We should bring more citizens under the coverage of old-age pensions and unemployment insurance.

We should widen the opportunities for adequate medical care.

We should plan a better system by which persons deserving or needing gainful employment may obtain it.

I have called for personal sacrifice. And I am assured of the willingness of almost all Americans to respond to that call.

A part of the sacrifice means the payment of more money in taxes. In my Budget Message I will recommend that a greater portion of this great defense program be paid for from taxation than we are paying for today. No person should try, or be allowed, to get rich out of the program; and the principle of tax payments in accordance with ability to pay should be constantly before our eyes to guide our legislation. If the Congress maintains these principles, the voters, putting patriotism ahead of pocketbooks, will give you their applause.

In the future days, which we seek to make secure, we look forward to a world founded upon four essential human freedoms.

The first is freedom of speech and expression—everywhere in the world.

The second is freedom of every person to worship God in his own way—everywhere in the world.

The third is freedom from want—which, translated into world terms, means economic understandings which will secure to every nation a healthy peacetime life for its inhabitants—everywhere in the world.

The fourth is freedom from fear—which, translated into world terms, means a world-wide reduction of armaments to such a point and in such a thorough fashion that no nation will be in a position to commit an act of physical aggression against any neighbor—anywhere in the world.

That is no vision of a distant millennium. It is a definite basis for a kind of world attainable in our own time and generation. That kind of world is the very antithesis of the so-called new order of tyranny which the dictators seek to create with the crash of a bomb. To that new order we oppose the greater conception—the moral order. A good society is able to face schemes of world domination and foreign revolutions alike without fear.

Since the beginning of our American history, we have been engaged in change—in a perpetual peaceful revolution—a revolution which goes on steadily, quietly adjusting itself to changing conditions—without the concentration camp or the quick-lime in the ditch. The world order which we seek is the cooperation of free countries, working together in a friendly, civilized society. This nation has placed its destiny in the hands and heads and hearts of its millions of free men and women; and its faith in freedom under the guidance of God. Freedom means the supremacy of human rights everywhere. Our support goes to those who struggle to gain those rights and keep them. Our strength is our unity of purpose.

To that high concept there can be no end save victory.

Source: *Congressional Record*, 77 Cong., 1 Sess., pp. 44–47.

Analysis

On January 6, 1941, President Franklin D. Roosevelt in his state of the Union Address to Congress outlined four fundamental freedoms that people "everywhere in the world" ought to enjoy. The four freedoms included freedom of speech and worship, and freedom from fear, and from want. Roosevelt delivered his speech 11 months before the United States declared war on Japan following the attack on Pearl Harbor on December 8, 1941. Roosevelt's speech was largely about the national security of the United States and the threat posed by aggressive dictatorships to other democracies. He referred to a "a moment unprecedented in the history of the Union" and warned the American people that "at no previous time has American security been as seriously threatened from without." The speech represented a break with the tradition of United States non-interventionism that had long been held in the United States. He outlined the U.S. role in helping allies already engaged in warfare and summarized the values of democracy behind the bipartisan consensus on international involvement that existed at the time. In an oblique reference to previous attempts by democracies to appease ruthless dictators, Roosevelt argued that "those, who would give up essential liberty to purchase a little temporary safety, deserve neither liberty nor safety." The president warned that "we may take pride in the fact that we are softhearted; but we cannot afford to be soft-headed" going on to claim that America's democratic values were directly assailed either by arms and aggression, or by the "secret spreading of poisonous propaganda."

Roosevelt appeared to be anticipating a forthcoming conflict and by enouncing these four key "freedoms," preparing the people for "total war." Unsurprisingly, the speech was heavily criticized by isolationists and many conservatives within Congress who argued against Roosevelt's attempt to justify and depict the war as necessary for the defense of liberal policies.[3]

A famous quote from the speech prefaces the values that America stands for: "As men do not live by bread alone, they do not fight by armaments alone." To this end, Roosevelt announced that he had asked Congress to fund the manufacture of additional armaments and supply's to those nations which "are now in actual war with aggressor nations."

Roosevelt referred to the speech as "unique in our history" and it unquestionably proved prescient; not only was American security breeched by the Japanese attack at Pearl Harbor—an unanticipated act of aggression that shocked the nation—but the four freedoms that the president outlined in his speech justified the United States entry into World War II and appealed to the nation's resolve once it declared war on Japan. In 1943 the artist, Norman Rockwell, in conjunction with the Office of War Information (OWI), produced a series of posters illustrating each of the four freedoms in a highly successful war-bond drive. Rockwell's Four Freedoms first appeared in four consecutive issues of the *Saturday Evening Post* starting on February 20, 1943. Each issue was accompanied with an essay by a handpicked writer who attempted to expound on the ideas Rockwell had depicted with his brush. Pulitzer Prize-winner Booth Tarkington wrote the accompanying text for Freedom of Speech. The historian Will Durant commented on Freedom of Worship. Carlos Bulosan, a Filipino immigrant, wrote the essay for Freedom from Want, and poet and OWI staffer Stephen Vincent Benét discussed Freedom from Fear.

The OWI made these posters the centerpiece of a war-bond drive in early 1943. Copies of them, accompanied by banners urging citizens to fight for the freedoms depicted, appeared in factories, offices, and stores throughout the country. The original art went on tour, too. The Four Freedoms War Bond Show traveled around the nation, appearing in major department stores. Many municipalities staged parades and appearances by celebrities to coincide with the show's arrival. The year-long campaign drew more than 1.2 million people and raised $132 million for the war effort. By the end of the war, 4 million posters had been printed. A series of postage stamps were also issued. The spirit of Roosevelt's propaganda message was encapsulated in Rockwell's *Save Freedom of Speech* painting and poster. An "ordinary Joe," with gnarled hands and in disheveled working clothes, speaks at a town hall meeting, his right to do so recognized in the apt attention of his fellow, middle-class citizens.[4]

Notes

1. The Munich crisis is forever associated with a policy of "appeasement" and British prime minister Neville Chamberlain's three meeting with Hitler in September 1938 to avert a war by conceding to German demands regarding Sudeten German in the independent state of Czechoslovakia.

2. Chatham House, also known as the Royal Institute of International Affairs, emerged out of the Paris Peace Conference (1919) and came into existence in 1920. As a nongovernmental organization based in London, its mission is to analyze and promote the understanding of major international issues and current affairs.

3. For a further discussion of these issue see, D. M. Kennedy, *Freedom from Fear: The American People in Depression and War, 1929–1945* (Oxford: Oxford University Press, 1999); and J. Bodnar, *The "Good War" in American Memory* (Maryland: Johns Hopkins University Press, 2010).

4. Revealingly, Rockwell's idealized images associated with the four freedoms are almost exclusively "white" (there appears to be one African American face on the outer edges of Freedom to Worship). In propaganda terms, this may seem surprising given that African Americans would be expected to fight for such "freedoms." See, T. Wright, *"The Depression and World War II." American Art and Artists* (HarperCollins, 2007), 122–123.

Chapter 2

Radio Propaganda:
When Hitler Speaks

When Joseph Goebbels became Minister for Propaganda in 1933, the news-paper and film industries were still privately owned; the broadcasting system, however, had been state-regulated since 1925. Although the Nazis had failed to gain access to this medium while in opposition, once in power the "coor-dination" of German radio proved comparatively easy. From the moment he assumed power, Goebbels recognized its propaganda potential and he was determined to make the most of this relatively new medium.

Poster art also played an important role in Nazi propaganda. Artists were commissioned to commemorate the more prestigious public works schemes that had been inspired by Hitler. The building of the Autobahns proved par-ticularly popular and figured heavily in state-sponsored art. Carl Protzen, for example, painted the grandiose building schemes in *The Führer's Roads* (1940). It is an appallingly poor and unimaginative painting and representative of the poverty of imagination that characterized art in the Third Reich. A number of artists worked on poster design—indeed, posters and paintings often comple-mented each other in the propaganda of the Third Reich. The manner in which the Nazis attempted to impress the importance of community radio listening illustrates this point.

The technical mobilization of German radio as the "voice of the nation" is a history of remarkable accomplishment, and it was the role of artists and poster designers to record such achievements. To increase the number of listeners, the Nazis persuaded manufacturers to produce one of the cheapest wireless sets in Europe, the VE 3031 or *Volksempfänger* ("people's receiver"). The "people's radio" was heavily subsidized so that it would be affordable to all workers. In fact, two versions of radio receivers were quickly produced: one for 75 Reich Marks and the *Volksempfänger* for 35RM payable in instalments. A famous poster issued by the Propaganda Ministry advertising the *Volksempfänger* showed one of these uniform radio sets surrounded by thousands of German citizens, with the caption proclaiming that *All Germany Listens to the Führer on the People's Receiver* (1936). Interestingly Hitler does not appear on the poster; instead, a huge crowd is gathered around a "people's radio" (*Reichsvolksemp-fänger*) listening intently to the words of their leader. The "people's radio" was designed with a limited range, which meant that Germans who purchased them were unable to receive foreign broadcasts. Great emphasis was placed on the encouragement of community listening with local party branches organizing such events. When a speech by Hitler or a leading Nazi figure or indeed an important announcement was to be made, the network of radio wardens established loudspeakers in public squares and staged what came to be referred to as "National Moments" (*Stunden der Nation*). The poster was used to encourage all Germans to buy one of these subsidized, uniform radio sets as an act of faith in the regime. One-and-a-half million sets were produced during 1933, and in 1934, the figure for radio sets had passed the 6 million mark. By the beginning of World War II, over 70 percent of households owned a radio—the highest percentage anywhere in the world.[1]

The poster, *All Germany Listens to the Führer*, captured in a crude, dramatic form the propaganda potential of the medium for the dissemination of National Socialist ideas and the importance attached to radio listening in the Third Reich. Artists on the other hand were expected to capture the *spirit* of community listening. A painting by the German artist Paul Mathias Padua showed, not a communal scene, but a typical extended peasant Aryan family (three generations) listening intently in their living room to the radio under the title *The Führer Speaks*. It is 1940, and Hitler is at the height of his popularity, boasting extraordinary blitzkrieg military victories in the West (commemorated by Padua in his *The 10th May 1940*, which celebrated the Germans' opening of the Western offensive). *The Führer Speaks* included not only the *Reichsvolksempfänger*, which is given pride of place in the room, but also featured a picture of Hitler on the wall to the left of the radio. So we have a painting within a painting that manages to capture the People's Community in an act of communal listening and at the same time links such activity with a timely reminder that is the towering figure of Adolf Hitler that remains at the pinnacle of the *Volksgemeinschaft* (People's Community). It represents, therefore, a carefully constructed snapshot of life in Nazi Germany in 1939/1940 and a further example of how painting contributed to the cultivation of the Führer cult. Its official seal of approval was recognized when the painting was exhibited at the Great German Art Exhibition in 1940.[2]

Document 3

J. B. PRIESTLEY, EXTRACT FROM HIS RADIO TALKS, *POSTSCRIPTS* (1940)

Document

5th June 1940

I wonder how many of you feel as I do about this great Battle and evacuation of Dunkirk. The news of it came as a series of surprises and shocks, followed by equally astonishing new waves of hope. What strikes me about it is how typically English it is. Nothing, I feel, could be more English both in its beginning and its end, its folly and its grandeur. We have gone sadly wrong like this before, and here and now we must resolve never, never to do it again. What began as a miserable blunder, a catalogue of misfortunes ended as an epic of gallantry. We have a queer habit—and you can see it running through our history—of conjuring up such transformations. And to my mind what was most characteristically English about it was the part played not by the warships but by the little pleasure-steamers. We've known them and laughed at them, these fussy little steamers, all our lives. These 'Brighton Belles' and 'Brighton Queens' left that innocent foolish world of theirs to sail into the inferno, to defy bombs, shells, magnetic mines, torpedoes, machine-gun fire—to rescue our soldiers.

21st July, 1940

We cannot go forward and build up this new world order, and this is our war aim, unless we begin to think differently one must stop thinking in terms of property and power and begin thinking in terms of community and creation. Take the change from property to community. Property is the old-fashioned way of thinking of a country as a thing, and a collection of things in that thing, all owned by certain people and constituting property; instead of thinking of a country as the home of a living society with the community itself as the first test . . .

And I'll give you an instance of how this change should be working. Near where I live is a house with a large garden, that's not being used at all because the owner of it has gone to America. Now, according to the property view, this is all right, and we, who haven't gone to America, must fight to protect this absentee owner's property. But on the community view, this is all wrong. There are hundreds of working men not far from here who urgently need ground for allotments so that they can produce a bit more food. Also, we may soon need more houses for billeting. Therefore, I say, that house and garden ought to be used whether the owner, who's gone to America, likes it or not.

Source: J. B. Priestley, *Postscripts* (Heinemann, London, 1940). Reprinted in J. B. Priestley, *All England Listened: The Wartime Broadcasts of J.B. Priestley* (Chilmark Press, London, 1968), 51–58. Permission granted by United Agents.

Analysis

Radio was the primary medium of mass communication in the 1930s, with radio sales booming during the Great Depression. Radio simultaneously emerged as a tool of mass persuasion and propaganda. On gaining power in 1933, the Nazis produced one of the cheapest wireless sets in Europe, the *Volksempfänger* ("people's receiver"). In addition to domestic broadcasts, the Nazi regime used the radio to deliver its message to both occupied territories and enemy states. One of the main targets was the United Kingdom to which William Joyce broadcast regularly, gaining him the nickname "Lord Haw-Haw" in the process. At the height of his influence, in 1940 Joyce had an estimated 6 million regular and 18 million occasional listeners in the United Kingdom. The broadcasts always began with the announcer's words "Germany calling, Germany calling, Germany calling." These broadcasts urged the British people to surrender and were well known for their jeering, sarcastic, and menacing tone.[3] Broadcasts were also made to the United States, notably through Robert Henry Best and "Axis Sally," Mildred Gillars. In Fascist Italy, Mussolini constructed his speeches around the medium of radio and insisted that his speeches were broadcast live to the Italian people. In the Soviet Union, radio offered both a means of communicating with the masses worldwide and a way of associating the Bolshevik cause with the technology of the future. To this end, Radio Moscow was founded in 1929 and caused a hurried response from the West.

In 1933, Franklin D. Roosevelt gave the first of his "fireside chats," which involved a more informal style of speaking than was common in the 1930s. Radio's influence peaked during World War II. The average American and British turned first to radio for war news. In the United States, popular commentators such as Edward R. Murrow, H. V. Kaltenborn, Elmer Davis, and Fulton Lewis Jr. gave listeners both the headlines plus their personal opinions—which were sometimes rather simplistic and biased!

The best example of this trend is the news reports of Edward Murrow. Murrow covered the Battle of Britain and particularly the nightly bombing raids on London. Murrow's inimitable style combined colorful imagery and sober reflection. The following is taken from his report ("I Am a Neutral Reporter") in November 1940, which also formed the basis of his commentary to the film *London (Britain) Can Take It*. By focusing on the common man and woman, Murrow wanted to let Americans know that England was fighting a "people's war," not a war for its colonies, as the American isolationists claimed:[4]

> I am a neutral reporter, I have watched the people of London live and die ever since death in its most ghastly garb began to come here as a nightly visitor five weeks ago. I have watched them stand by their homes. I have seen them made homeless. I have seen them move to new homes. And I can assure you that there is no panic, no fear, no despair in London town; there is nothing but determination, confidence and high courage among the people of Churchill's island.[5]

Radio broadcasting played a crucial role both in government propaganda and within the context of the broader cultural and political transformation of wartime America. During the war, Americans' already heavy reliance on the radio was heightened and intensified. More than 90 percent of American families owned at least one radio set and listened to it, on average, for about four hours daily. News programs and political talk shows accounted for just over 5 percent of the program schedule in the late 1930s, but their share increased to almost 20 percent by the mid-1940s.[6] While the Roosevelt administration supervised specific radio propaganda series during these years, a significant participation occurred through the integration of propaganda into established shows such as the radio soap operas and the popular comedy programs of Jack Benny and Bob Hope. As the war progressed, propaganda campaigns exhorting the American people to make the necessary sacrifices were increasingly dominated by the private corporate sector.[7]

In Britain, BBC speakers, often supplied by arrangement with the Ministry of Information, were under attack during the early stage of the war. Home Intelligence reports, frequently drew attention to the fact that many poorer people "find wireless voices too impersonal and language too academic to affect them personally."[8] Hence, the great popularity of J. B. Priestley's broadcasts. Priestley was a well-known writer and dramatist; he was a celebrant of the English countryside and a devotee of the English national character. His popularity increased when the BBC began a series of *Postscript* to the Nine O'clock news. The *Postscripts*, broadcast on Sunday night through 1940 and again in 1941, drew peak audiences of 16 million; only Churchill was more popular with listeners.

During a five-month period from June to October 1940, J. B. Priestley made a series of 10-minute broadcasts on Sunday nights for the BBC General Overseas service titled *Postscripts*. He recorded his impressions of the developing conflict, while at the same time describing the changing scenes around him—the armies preparing for war, the once-teeming streets of London now deserted, the crowds of women and children at the mainline railway stations preparing for evacuation. The radio broadcasts made him into a media celebrity. He was already a household name, thanks to his best-selling novel *The Good Companions* (1929), his time plays, his prolific journalism, and his observations on the social problems he witnessed in *English Journey* (1934). But the *Postscripts* brought Priestley's reassuring Yorkshire voice into millions of homes, bringing encouragement and inspiration at an incredibly dangerous, difficult, and heightened time.

During the Dunkirk crisis, the Government and the BBC, fearing a failure of lower-class morale, turned to Priestley as the ideal communicator with ordinary people. His warm, Yorkshire tones contrasted strongly with the public school accents usually heard on radio. Priestley proved to be an enormous success, gave 19 postscripts between June and October and received over 1,600 letters a week from the public.[9]

J.B. Priestley made his first *Postscripts* broadcast on Wednesday June 5, 1940, the day after the end of Operation Dynamo, the evacuation of British and French troops from the beaches of Dunkirk by British destroyers and assorted small craft (see Document 10). In this broadcast, Priestley took the raw stuff of news and played a part in turning it into history, or legend. "Doesn't it seem to you to have an inevitable air about it—as if we had turned a page in the history of Britain and seen a chapter headed 'Dunkirk'?" From the outset, he assumed he and his listeners were in the same situation: "I wonder how many of you feel as I do about this great Battle and evacuation of Dunkirk?" Priestley emphasized how typically English that "a miserable blunder, a catalogue of misfortunes and miscalculations, ended as an epic of gallantry." He contrasted this with the German approach, which would never make such mistakes, but would never rise to such heights of courage. "This is not the German way," he explained, for the Germans would never make such mistakes because they are machines without souls. He did not dwell on the blunder, or try to apportion blame. Instead, he sought to inspire his listeners by paying tribute to the little ships, especially the pleasure steamers. He evoked a shared world, of an English sea-side, "pierrots and piers, sand castles, ham-and-egg teas, palmists, automatic machines, and crowded sweating promenades." The steamers had left this "ridiculous holiday world" to sail into "the inferno . . . to rescue our soldiers." Some would not come back but would be remembered forever, like *Gracie Fields*, a ship Priestley had taken many times to his Isle of Wight home. *Gracie Field* was a popular entertainer and the darling of Lancashire. Operation Dynamo had naturally concentrated on the ports of southeastern England, but by shrewdly referring to *Gracie Fields*, Priestley had incorporated northern England into the narrative.

For Priestley, only the British could have come up with Dunkirk, when triumph was snatched from defeat. He brilliantly turned Dunkirk into an inspiring epic by emphasizing the polarity between the real role of the little ships and their employment in the evacuation. Such acts of bravery would allow Britain to fight another day. Priestley came across as a man of the people, who shunned the political or military aspects of the war, and talked rather about the efforts of ordinary men and women to survive setbacks. These people are the heroes of total war and such national character traits will, he guarantees, secure ultimate victory. He ended this broadcast on a defiant note: "And our great grand-children when they learn how we began this War by snatching glory out of defeat, and then swept on to victory, may also learn how the little holiday steamers made an excursion to hell and came back glorious." Priestley's broadcast extols the virtues of the British people as a prelude to exhorting them to expend greater effort in continuance of the war, if the nation is to survive.

In the *Postscripts* broadcast dated July 7, 1940, Priestley described the tranquil scene around him during the so-called phoney war, (Cf. Document 37) which led him on to reflect on Winston Churchill's suitability as a war leader to nullify the threat of the "evil magician" Adolf Hitler. In another broadcast dated July 28, 1940, he mused about the aircrew risking their lives to save world once the conflict had ended. He reflected on the emotions experienced by those left at home, as their partners flew off to fight the Nazis. Given the sacrifices they were making, Priestley hoped that the postwar world would be one they could enjoy; that it would not be the same as in 1918, when service personnel returned to a Britain which could offer them nothing—no jobs, no prospects, no financial security. On August 4, he reflected more on the social and cultural changes Britain had experienced since 1914; the people had undergone the Depression; now they were fighting a new kind of war—total war. However, he fervently believed that they would gain renewed strength through the experience; unlike the Nazis who suffered under a totalitarian regime, the British had the prospect of freedom to look forward to.

Priestley was an old-fashioned socialist in the sense that he hoped that a brave new world would emerge from the conflict—a classless society devoted to equality of opportunity for men and women alike, where the old social hierarchies would be destroyed. In this world, people would take care of each other: the snobbery that dominated pre-1939 Britain (especially amongst the middle classes) could no longer return, particularly after the experience of war, where everybody looked out for one another's interests. In many ways, his political views anticipated those of the Labour Party in the post-1945 period, which created the welfare state in an attempt to fulfil these objectives. Perhaps, not surprisingly, his talks were eventually cancelled. It was thought that this was the effect of complaints from the cabinet that they were too left-wing. Nevertheless, Priestley, like other radio broadcasters such as Ed Murrow and Lord Haw-Haw demonstrated the power of radio as a powerful propaganda medium. In the case of Priestley and his *Postscripts*, these broadcasts kept citizens informed about the war efforts and helped keep the spirits of Britain high during a time of hardship. The British wartime radio landscape would never be the same again.[10]

Notes

1. For a further discussion see, D. Welch, *The Third Reich. Politics and Propaganda* (London: Routledge, 2002), 38–43.

2. For a wider, critical analysis of the arts in Nazi Germany see, P. Adam, *The Arts of the Third Reich* (London: Thames & Hudson, 1992).

3. Cf. M. Doherty, *Nazi Wireless Propaganda* (Edinburgh: Edinburgh University Press, 2000).

4. Murrow believed official news was less important than the more intimate stories of human sacrifice. Regarding his radio broadcast he explained that a night with London's fire fighters "brought the war much nearer to the wheat farmer in Kansas than any official communiqué." Quoted in R. F. Smith, *Edward R. Murrow: The War Years* (Michigan: New Issues Press, 1978), 56.

5. Ministry of Information film *London Can Take It* (1940); commentary reprinted in *Documentary News Letter*, November 1940, 6–7.

6. G. Horten, *Radio Goes to War. The Cultural Politics of Propaganda during World War II* (California: University of California Press, 2002).

7. For a fuller discussion see, Horten, *Radio Goes to War*.

8. Home Intelligence Daily Reports, June 15, 1940, INF 1/264.

9. Cited in M. Connelly, *We Can Take It! Britain and the Memory of the Second World War* (London: Pearson, 2004), 75.

10. Goebbels took Priestley's impact seriously, referring to him in his diary as "the English radio spokesman . . . spouting the most outrageous nonsense against us on the radio." F. Taylor (ed.), *The Goebbels Diaries, 1939–1941* (London: Hamish Hamilton, 1982) entry for March 4, 1942, 254.

Chapter 3
America Enters the War

OPENING SCENES FROM THE *WHY WE FIGHT* DOCUMENTARY SERIES (1942–1945)

Document

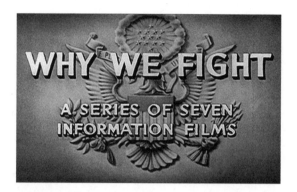

Source: National Archives.

Analysis

In his State of the Union address to Congress and later in the year his war message on December 8, 1941, President Roosevelt declared that Americans, although in grave danger, had determination and a confidence in defending the nation's cherished values. Although these speeches proved inspirational once the United States became embroiled in war, in 1941 most Americans wanted to stay out of the conflict already under way in Europe and Asia. Many believed that the lessons of World War I was to avoid other people's wars. Shocked and angered, they now found themselves in a war for which they were not prepared. What had been the origins of the war, where was it going, and how would it end? It was one of the responsibilities of wartime propaganda to answer these questions in a way that would mobilize the population for total war.[1]

In essence, the war would be justified as a fight for freedom. American propaganda drew on FDR's "four freedoms." Winning the war meant defeating the "new order of tyranny" of the Axis with its dictators, bombs, concentration camps, and "quick-lime in the ditch." Winning the peace meant establishing a new world order of "cooperation of free countries" based on the four freedoms (see Document 2).

One of the most interesting examples of official propaganda justifying the war *Why We Fight*, a series of seven documentary films commissioned by the United States government, whose purpose was to show American soldiers the reason for U.S. involvement in the war. Later on, they were also shown to the general public to persuade them to support American involvement in the war.

At the onset of war, the U.S. Army recognized the need to foster and maintain morale and this interest was now allied with the "science" of public relations and behavioral psychology. The result was a dramatic propaganda experiment in what is referred to by one historian, as "social engineering for a democracy at war."[2] Crucial to the work of troop indoctrination was General George C. Marshall, Army Chief of Staff, who fervently believed in the power of educational film. Marshall was dissatisfied with existing methods of troop indoctrination consisting largely of mandatory orientation talks.

Hollywood's Frank Capra received the assignment to make the *Why We Fight* series. Capra had enjoyed a string of commercial success including *It Happened One Night* (1934), *Mr. Deeds Goes to Town* (1936), and *Mr. Smith Goes to Washington* (1939)—films that identified with the American dream and the little guy. In 1940, Capra had accepted a reserve commission in the Army Signal Corps. The result was seven completed films that attempted to justify American participation as unavoidable. Facts were selected with an eye to offering emotional reasons for supporting one's own war effort; the cause of one's allies; and for fearing and hating one's enemies. In order of distribution they were

> *Prelude to War* (1942) examines the difference between democratic and fascist states;

> *The Nazi Strike* (1943) covers the Nazi conquest of Europe through *Blitzkrieg*;

Divide and Conquer (1943), which attributed the collapse of France to Fifth Columnists;

The Battle of Britain (1943) depicts Britain's victory against the Luftwaffe;

The Battle of Russia (1943) shows a history of Russian defense and Russia's battle against Germany;

The Battle of China (1944) shows Japan's attempts to conquer China and control Asia;

War Comes to America (1945) similar to *Prelude* but more concerned with tracing shifts in American attitudes from isolationism to interventionism.[3]

The first of the *Why We Fight* series, the Academy award-winning *Prelude to War*, established a style that characterized most of Capra's wartime work: lengthy voice-over narration, rapid montage, stirring music, and dramatic animations sequences created by Walt Disney productions. The *Why We Fight* series were in essence compilation films that used newsreels, captured enemy footage, and other stock film sources as their raw material. Visually they resembled the *March of Time* format that had been developed in America in the 1930s.

Prelude to War describes World War II as a battle between the "slave world" of fascism and the "free world" of American liberty. In the "slave world," the entire populations of Germany, Italy, and Japan have been hoodwinked by madmen, opportunists who capitalized on their people's desperation and weakness to rise to power. These demagogues promised revenge for past losses, and in the process convinced their people to give up their rights and accept dictatorship. In the "free world," the principles of equality, freedom, and liberty characterize the greatest leaders, embodied in the works and words of Washington, Jefferson, and Lincoln. This freedom is a threat to the fascist dictators of the Axis powers, which claim that democracy is weak and must be eradicated. The film claims that the ultimate goal of the Axis powers is to enslave the nations of the "free world," a desire made manifest in the Japanese invasion of Manchuria and Mussolini's destruction of Ethiopia.

The *Why We Fight* series were mandatory viewing for all military personnel in 1942 and soldiers had their personal log book stamped to show that they had seen the films.

Prelude to War, the most successful of the seven films, was shown to President Roosevelt who believed it was so important that he ordered it to be shown to the general public. It won the Academy Award for best documentary in 1942. Eventually three of the series found commercial distribution within the United States. Worldwide distribution followed with foreign language soundtracks. In Britain, Prime Minister Winston Churchill wanted to see the series widely distributed, but the Ministry of Information's Film Division disliked it and attempted to restrict circulation. At least 54 million Americans had seen the series by the end of the war, and studies were done to gauge the impact of the films.[4] The *Why We Fight* series provides the most comprehensive statement of American war aims to military and civilian audiences with a clarity that Roosevelt's four freedoms never could. The series demonstrated that, skillfully used, the medium of film could motivate the public and boost morale.

Notes

1. See, S. Brewer, "Fighting for Freedom: The Second World War and a Century of American War Propaganda," in D. Welch and J. Fox (eds.), *Justifying War. Propaganda, Politics and the Modern Age* (Basinstoke: Palgrave, 2012), 218–235.

2. D. Culbert, "'Why We Fight': Social Engineering for a Democratic Society at War," in K.R.M Short (ed.), *Film and Radio Propaganda in World War II* (London: Croom Helm, 1983), 173–191.

3. The documentary actually uses Gallop Poll data to document graphically changes in public opinion. At least 3.74 million people had seen it by July 1, 1945. Culbert, (1983), 184.

4. J. Combs and S. Combs, *Film Propaganda and American Politics: An Analysis and Filmography* (New York: Garland Publishing, Inc., 1994).

Chapter 4

The Poster

All the belligerents stressed the central message that citizens had a crucial role contributing to the war effort. In Britain, as we have seen, the theme of "your country needs you" manifested itself in a shared "people's war" working together in a common cause to fight Nazism. However, the strategy initially pursued by the Ministry of Information began disastrously. It adopted a stance of exhortation that was reflected in the poster "*Your* Courage, *Your* Cheerfulness, *Your* Resolution WILL BRING US VICTORY." This merely served to create an "us" and "them" attitude, the folly of which was soon pointed out by the intelligence reports. The MOI quickly learned its mistake and citizens were encouraged to put aside class and regional differences and "Go Forward Together" with the Prime Minister Winston Churchill and the armed forces (interestingly the navy does not appear in the poster). Government exhortations quickly multiplied as "total war" required ever more urgent calls for citizens to "fall-in" and participate in the war effort ("We're Going to See It Through").

British citizens could not avoid Ministry of Information propaganda campaigns on large street boardings urging them to—among other things—walk, dig for victory, save money, join the forces, and save on coal. Women (two of whom can be seen walking past the posters) were often the main targets for this advice. Both government and commercial posters became a ubiquitous presence and transformed the "everyday" experience and industrial landscape of ordinary people engaged in "total war."

In 1939, posters were less important to the belligerent governments than in 1914. During World War I, posters and newspapers together with pamphlets and the new medium of film made up the means of mass communication. By 1939, the print media no longer dominated but shared the field equally with radio, films, and newsreels. Nevertheless, the intense politicization of the poster during the 1930s by totalitarian regimes inevitably made it an important presence in a conflict that was more ideological than World War I. Industrialisation during the 19th century had utilized posters for mass persuasion and this had proved extremely effective. Posters contained numerous advantages; they were relatively cheap to produce, they had been tried and tested, and they were a medium accepted and understood by the masses. In World War II therefore posters were an obvious means of communications to disseminate propaganda and all governments continued to rely heavily on the poster to put across its wartime messages.

The themes disseminated were very much dictated by the course of the war. Governments exploited posters for recruitment, requests for war loans, to make national policies acceptable, to encourage industrial effort, to urge conservation of resources and inform the public of food and fuel substitutes, and to channel emotions such as courage and hatred. Remember although we are viewing these posters in isolation, they were employed as a part of a bigger war effort campaign, together with personal appearances by celebrities, pageants, house-to-house calls, popular songs, and flag days.

Document 5
"REMEMBER DEC. 7TH!" (USA, 1941)

Document

Source: Library of Congress.

Analysis

Posters were also used to justify the war. Perhaps the most successful example of this is "Remember Dec. 7th!" (USA, 1941) where, a poster skillfully exploits the emotional associations with the national flag. Perhaps the most striking symbol of nationhood is the national flag. In the United States, for example, the idea of the flag is fundamental to the Oath of Allegiance: "I pledge allegiance to the Flag of the United States of America, and to the Republic for which it stands, one Nation under God, indivisible, with liberty and justice for all." In times of war or other crises, citizens are encouraged to "rally around the flag"; in times of national elation such as a sporting event, the national flag becomes the proud symbol of prowess.

Flags represent a powerful force that cements people together; but, conversely, for those who are not included they can foster a sense of isolation and "apartness." On the one hand, such symbols may simply represent the visible part of an accepted, and acceptable, patriotism—the simple expression of national identity; on the other hand, they can be a dangerous component of ideological doctrine and a powerful weapon of a regime's propaganda, perhaps the most obvious example being the Nazi swastika.

Document 5 is a patriotic U.S. poster from World War II. To galvanize the rage that Americans felt after the Japanese attack on Pearl Harbor, the Office of War Information US government produced this in 1942, one of the most stirring propaganda posters ever made. Designed by Allen Saalburg, it unites a determination to "Remember Dec. 7th" with expressions of resolve from President Lincoln's Gettysburg Address ("we here highly resolve that these dead shall not have died in vain . . ."). With the haunting image of a tattered Stars and Stripes swaying against a burning black sky, it perfectly captured the emotion of its intended audience.

Posters of World War II generally contained more realistic images of life at both the fighting and home fronts. Germany, Italy, and Japan used atrocity propaganda extensively. By accusing the enemy of crimes may well have helped justify one's own atrocities. Britain and the United States, on the other hand, rarely stressed atrocities. Reaction to jingoistic propaganda was sharp in Britain. One working man in 1940 spoke for many when he said of patriotic posters then issued: "That flag-waving won't carry anymore. The present posters are old fashioned. Need something which gives us more news or cartoons. Cheer us up a bit, there's no community spirit without that."[1] In Britain, the public had grown more sceptical as a result of atrocity propaganda disseminated during World War I and it was no longer considered an effective theme. As a result, humor was more generally employed in World War II, possibly because the civilian morale demanded tonics such as "Fougasse's" (Cyril Kenneth Bird) deflating poster images of Hitler and Göring or Tommy Handley's popular radio program, *It's That Man Again*. Production posters in factories often contained a humorous approach; as did posters intended to prevent accidents, promote salvage, or encourage healthier eating and public hygiene (see Documents 9 and 19). The malicious squander bug helped the German war effort by encouraging the British housewife to spend her money on luxuries, just as the Tokio Kid in America helped Japan by encouraging careless talk and absenteeism (see Document 42).

Note

1. Quoted in J. Darracott and B. Lotus, *Second World War Posters* (London: Imperial War Museum, 1972), 6. See also, P. Paret, B. Irwin Lewis, and P. Paret, *Persuasive Images. Posters of War and Revolution* (Princeton, NJ: Princeton University Press, 1992), 142–213.

Chapter 5
The Propaganda of Leadership

"ADOLF HITLER IS VICTORY!" (R. GERHARD ZILL, 1943)

Document

Source: Poster by R. Gerhard Zill. Photo by Galerie Bilderwelt/Getty Images.

Analysis

Charismatic Leadership

This document is a painting of Adolf Hitler by R. Gerhard Zill, who specialized in capturing the German leader and aspects of German life from a Nazi perspective. It was commissioned shortly after the Nazis had experienced their first major military setback at Stalingrad and represented an attempt by Joseph Goebbels, the minister for propaganda, to reassure the population that victory was still assured. It is particularly interesting because it illustrates a wider aspect of propaganda in World War II, namely the importance of political leadership.

In the 20th century, the personality cults attached to national leaders were not in themselves new phenomena; but the arrival of the mass media, in conjunction with the rise of communist and fascist states, highlighted them as a means to legitimize regimes. Dictators seeking to alter or transform their nations according to radical ideas have invariably used the mass media and propaganda to create idealized, heroic public images of themselves. Such an approach to leadership has been defined by Max Weber as "charismatic authority," and the cult of the leader, surpassing any normal level of trust in political leadership, is central to an understanding of the appeal of dictatorships—of both the Right and the Left—and is undoubtedly the most important theme cementing their propaganda together.[1]

Certainly, propaganda plays an important role in the projection of all leader figures. But at the head of a dictatorship stands a usually charismatic leader embodying the nation's will and aspirations. Italy's Benito Mussolini, a former journalist, was arguably the first fascist dictator to appreciate the value of propaganda and the tools of paramilitary display—uniforms, flags, parades (along with his frenzied balcony speeches)—to create a sense of belonging among his followers. Once he was in power, Italian propaganda depicted Il Duce as a protean superman whose powers were unlimited. Mussolini was well aware of the importance of the role and played up to such an image. He despised what he considered to be the effete liberal Italy that had emerged in the late 19th century and longed for the glories of ancient Rome. In a series of impassioned speeches he offered his countrymen the possibility of a Third Roman Empire, in which he would perpetuate the glorious tradition of the Roman emperors.

Italian Fascism claimed to be a movement of youth. In fact, it established a multiplicity of organizations for every age group. When the Fascists took office in Italy, they immediately reformed the school and university curricula, emphasizing Italy's role in world affairs, the importance of strong leadership and the need for discipline and sacrifice. One of the most popular propaganda posters of the time showed Mussolini in a formal Fascist paramilitary uniform. The bombastic pose was struck in countless newsreels and photographs and at national rallies—chin and stomach out, arm outstretched demanding authority from above and obedience from below, the whole summed up in the poster's slogan: "Believe/Obey/Fight."

When Adolf Hitler came to power in Germany in 1933, he promised the German people that the Nazi Reich would last a thousand years. A propaganda slogan of the period called upon the nation "to awake" (*Deutschland Erwache!*). Just as National Socialism needed its enemies, so it also required its heroes. For their concept of the heroic leader the Nazis turned to the German *völkisch* ("racial") philosophy of 19th-century Romanticism and the notion of the "leadership principle" (*Führerprinzip*), centered on a mystical figure embodying and guiding the nation's destiny in a similar fashion to Il Duce. The leadership principle required a very special personality, who had the will and power to actualize the "racial state" (*Volkstaat*), a man of destiny—resolute, dynamic, and radical—who would destroy the old privileged and class-ridden society and replace it with the ethnically pure and socially harmonious "national community" (*Volksgemeinschaft*). Hitler's tenure on absolute power was therefore justified not so much by virtue of his constitutional position as chancellor and head of state but more in charismatic terms as Führer of the German Volk—not a state, but a German nation as a racially determined entity. As the custodian of the nation's will, Hitler's authority eschewed constitutional limitations. The "Heil Hitler!" greeting would subsequently replace, by law, the traditional greeting GutenTag! Adults were made to greet each other with the new acclamation, and children in school used it at the start of each new lesson. It was accompanied by the familiar, stiff right-arm salute.

Like Italian Fascism, National Socialism demanded authority from above and obedience from below. A famous poster of the period showed Hitler in Renaissance pose above the propaganda slogan "One People, One Nation, One Leader!" ("Ein Volk, Ein Reich, Ein Führer!"). Other slogans included "The Hand That Guides the Reich," "Youth Serves the Führer," and "Hitler Is Victory." The creation of the Führer myth turned Hitler into the most vital legitimizing force within the regime, and in doing so bestowed upon him the halo of infallibility.

In cultivating the Führer cult, the depiction of Hitler was both essential and sensitive. While photographs of Hitler appeared regularly in the German press and provided the day-to-day contact between leader and people, artists, filmmakers, poets, and musicians were commissioned to depict Hitler in a more stylized fashion illustrating different aspects of the Führer's work, his moods, and his genius. Whatever form chosen, it would have to accord with official Nazi art policy.

Hitler's standing amongst the population reached its highest point with the signing of the armistice with France on June 22, 1940. If ever there was widespread enthusiasm for the war in Germany, then this was probably the period when it existed. It even overshadowed the general discontent felt about the coal shortages and the workings of the rationing system. The Secret Police Reports (SD Reports) claimed that the military victories had integrated the population behind Hitler's war aims: ". . . as a consequence of the military victories, an unprecedented solidarity has developed between the front and the domestic population, as well as unprecedented solidarity amongst the whole population."[2] Seduced by military conquest supported by propaganda, German public opinion appeared to have been convinced that Hitler was in command of the situation and that final victory seemed assured.

From the end of 1942 (i.e., before defeat at Stalingrad) a different, more sober image of Hitler began to emerge. After the surrender of the German Sixth Army at Stalingrad in January 1943, Hitler retreated into an increasingly illusory world and refused to speak to his people. The rare public appearances of Hitler meant that Goebbels worked harder than ever to maintain the Führer myth. Revealingly, Hitler's reluctance to address the nation was not compensated by an increase in Hitler iconography. In fact by the end of 1943, the Führer cult almost disappeared in terms of new images or propaganda slogans. There are few examples of state-commissioned art at the time presenting Hitler in a new and revitalized light. This cannot be explained solely by the exigencies of war as the Propaganda Ministry was spending huge amounts of money on other projects and campaigns. In May 1943, the Propaganda Office of the Party suggested a new slogan for a poster campaign, "The Führer Is Always Right," which was not taken up. Instead, the artist R. Gerhard Zill painted a half portrait of Hitler with a look of heroic fortitude standing in shadow by a chair with the slogan "Adolf Hitler Is Victory" ("Hitler ist der Sieg"). The title is separate and positioned across the bottom edge, in white, set against a black background, and Hitler is dressed in a naval-style jacket and medals. Released shortly after the disaster of Stalingrad, this painting became the most widely distributed poster of the Führer in the final period of the war.

In the summer of 1944, the intelligence reports confirmed a short-lived revival of trust in the Führer, following the failure of the July 20 plot against him. By portraying the Officer's Plot as a cowardly, unpatriotic act, Goebbels organized well-attended demonstrations of "spontaneous expression of the views of our people about the foul attempt on the Fuhrer's life."[3] The propaganda minister exploited the attempted assassination to show that the hand of providence was guiding Hitler by resurrecting the slogan "Hitler Is Victory." In the final year of the war, Goebbels attempted to breathe new life into the Führer-cult by depicting Hitler as a latter-day Frederick the Great, ultimately triumphant in the face of adversity. However, the overwhelming majority of the population now accepted that the war was irretrievably lost. Hitler no longer addressed the nation, he had virtually disappeared from the cinema screens, and the rare photographs that had escaped the censor revealed his declining physical and mental state. Even as late as April 29, 1945, the day before Hitler committed suicide in his bunker, a Berlin newspaper was still insisting that Hitler would remain steadfast with his people and "wherever the Führer is, there is victory." With Berlin about to fall, no amount of propaganda could sustain such an alarming flight from reality. The "Hitler myth" and the Third Reich were on the verge of extinction.

VASILY SELIVANOV, "GLORY TO OUR GREAT PEOPLE, A VICTORIOUS NATION!" (1945)

Document

Source: National Library of Russia.

Analysis

Compared to Hitler, Joseph Stalin's infallibility took rather longer to cultivate within the Soviet Union. When Lenin died in January 1924, it was widely believed that Leon Trotsky would take over as leader, but a complex power struggle developed from which Stalin finally emerged as undisputed leader by 1929. One could say that creation of the image began when—to use his real, Georgian name—Joseph Djugashvili took the name "Stalin," meaning "man of steel," some time after joining the Bolsheviks in 1904. But the Stalin cult is generally thought to have taken off in a significant way on the occasion of his 50th birthday in December 1929, when Soviet cities were decorated with flags, portraits, banners, and balloons, and tributes were widely paid to the rapidly emerging "leader of the international proletariat." As the first statues of him began to be commissioned, the new slogans became "Stalin Is the Lenin of Today" and "Stalin, Man of Steel."

Stalinist policies included the fostering of "socialism in one country," rapid industrialization, a centralized state, the collectivization of agriculture, and the subordination of interests of other communist parties to those of the Soviet Party. Stalin insisted that rapid industrialization was needed because the country was economically backward in comparison with others, and that it was needed in order to challenge internal and external enemies of communism. And industrial transformation was the overriding aim of the series of Five-Year Plans. The first (1928–1932) concentrated on heavy industry as did the second (1933–1937), which also provided for increases in consumer goods. Realizing (and surpassing) production targets became as much a psychological stimulus, a promise of better things to come, as an opportunity to show solidarity with the party and its leader. Propaganda eulogizing the achievements of the regime had an important function in mobilizing enthusiasm and pride in the modernization of Russia. Posters in particular had a significant role to play, carrying exhortations to workers: "Work, Build, and No Complaining," "Let's Storm the Production Targets!," or—in reference to the prize-winning and target-exceeding miner Aleksei Stakhanov—"Long Live the Stalinist Order of Heroes and Stakhanovites!" In the arts, "Socialist Realism," supposed to serve political imperatives, became the order of the day. Heroic, optimistic images intended to mirror everyday life were a feature of Soviet art in the 1930s and part of the wider cultural revolution that Stalin forced through as an important corollary of economic changes. Ritual gratitude was often in evidence ("Thanks to the Party, Thanks to Dear Stalin for a Happy, Joyful Childhood"). It should always be remembered that the propaganda was supplemented with a large dose of terror and coercion.

In 1936, in the midst of the purges that constituted the so-called Great Terror, a new Soviet constitution was introduced, which gave the illusion of being more democratic. While Karl Marx's "dictatorship of the proletariat" remained enshrined in it, in practice Stalin now assumed more power than Lenin had ever had. Thus, although Stalin still needed the memory of Lenin to provide ideological legitimacy for his actions, the cult of personality was such that he could now rewrite Soviet history in his own image.

It was, however, only during and after World War II—in Soviet parlance, the Great Patriotic War—that Stalin's image displaced that of Lenin, the "father of the revolution." The purges had stripped the Soviet Union of its political and military leadership, and the regime's triumphalist rhetoric had left the state unprepared for the Nazi invasion. The "Great Patriotic War" began disastrously. Nonetheless, Stalin showed considerable leadership qualities by personally directing the defense of the USSR. To increase popular enthusiasm for the war, Stalin reshaped his domestic policies to heighten the patriotic spirit. Nationalistic slogans and appeals for patriotic unity replaced much of the communist rhetoric in official pronouncements and the mass media ("Stalin in the Kremlin Cares for Each of Us," 1940). The endurance of the cities of Leningrad and Stalingrad became physical embodiments of Stalin's will to resist—and thus propaganda gifts reinforcing the Soviet Union's moral right to victory. In 1944, Vladimir Serov (1910–1968) produced a poster titled "Stalin Leads Us to Victory," which anticipated ultimate victory over Nazism. In the poster, Stalin's outstretched arm urges the nations and particularly the Soviet armed forces for one final push to victory.

After Stalingrad, the Soviet Union held the initiative for the rest of the war. By the end of 1943, the Red Army had broken through the German siege of Leningrad and recaptured much of the Ukrainian Republic. With decisive military superiority, Soviet forces drove into eastern Germany, capturing Berlin in May 1945. As victory seemed assured, the need for celebratory propaganda became apparent. Yelizaveta Svilova (1900–1975) directed the film *Berlin*, representing a compilation of the work of Soviet army cameramen, which was released in June 1945 as part of the victory celebrations. In the same period, artist and journalist, Vasily Selivanov (1902–1982), captured the joy of ultimate victory in his poster "Glory to Our Great People, a Victorious Nation!"[4] In Document 7, although the text is sparse, the visual content contains the trials and tribulations of the Soviet Union during World War II: the besieged Soviet cities, the brave Red Army, the mass of the Soviet people (depicted in photo-montage), and above all, the father of the nation, Stalin (in the form of the Stalin medal—one of the highest accolades bestowed during World War II). The medal with the resolute figure of Stalin reads in idiomatic Russian: "Our task is right" . . . . "We conquered." The poster by Selivanov (one of many that Soviet artists were commissioned to undertake), represents the high point of Stalin's cult, the culmination of his dictatorial infallibility. In the immediate aftermath of the war, Stalin was able to take credit for the defeat of Nazism and the emergence of the Soviet Union as a "superpower" with an unprecedented empire in Eastern Europe.

The propaganda of personality cults may loom large in totalitarian states, where leaders have sought to impose revolutionary ideas and change on a nation. But leader figures can assume extraordinary and charismatic impact in the history of democratic nations too. One only has to think of Winston Churchill's wartime premiership.

Churchill was a consummate propagandist and notable wordsmith, but he is said to have preferred deeds to words. After the resignation of Neville

Chamberlain as prime minister in the spring of 1940, Churchill rallied the British nation with his leadership and particularly the radio broadcasts of his speeches, which expressed the defiant spirit of the nation following the fall of France in June 1940: "We will fight them on the beaches; we will fight them in the fields and on the landing grounds, and we will never surrender." Churchill's bulldog appearance was a gift to propagandists and he played up to this by adopting a characteristic "V" for victory hand gesture. The bulldog symbol was revived from World War I and superimposed with Churchill's face. Posters (Cf. "Holding the Line" Henri Guignon, USA, 1942) and cartoonists ("Go To It," Sidney Strube, *Daily Express*, June 8, 1940.) widely used the Churchill bulldog in propaganda to signify British determination and tenacity. The war was Churchill's stage, and it was a case of "cometh the hour cometh the man"; as war drew to a close, he was unceremoniously voted out of office, suggesting the limitations of leader figures in democracies. Looking back on the war period at the end of his life, he commented that "the British people were the lion . . . I just provided the roar."

Notes

1. For a further discussion of the concept of strong leadership and propaganda in the 20th and 21st centuries see, D. Welch, *Propaganda Power and Persuasion* (London: British Library, 2013), 41–76.

2. The role of Adolf Hitler in Nazi propaganda is a theme I have taken up elsewhere. Cf. D. Welch, "'Working Towards the Führer': Charismatic Leadership and the Image of Adolf Hitler in Nazi Propaganda," in A. McElligott and Tim Kirk (eds.), *Working Towards the Führer* (Manchester: Manchester University Press, 2003), 93–117.

3. Cited in J. Noakes, *Nazism 1919–1945*, vol. 4: *The German Home Front in World War II* (Exeter: Exeter University Press, 1998), 548–549

4. Selivanov, became during the course of the war, editor and main artist of the Leningrad bureau of TASS Windows and some of his posters contained verses by the renowned Soviet poetess Vera Inber. His earlier works focused on the heroism of the besieged people of Leningrad and the brutality of Nazism.

Chapter 6

The Myth of Dunkirk

Winston Churchill called it "a miracle of deliverance." Only eight months after World War II had begun, the British army faced annihilation. On May 10, 1940, the day Churchill became the prime minister—the Germans invaded Holland, Belgium, and France. The British army had been fighting the Germans in France but was on the retreat and Churchill faced the possibility that they would be trapped ("Nothing but a miracle can save the BEF now," wrote General Brooke in his diary). On May 19 (when advancing German army had severed the main lines of communication between BEF and French headquarters), the commander of the BEF, Lord John Gort, decided that evacuation was the only way to save the British army. Without informing his allies—the French—he ordered the BEF to withdraw to Dunkirk and asked the British government to evacuate it by sea.

In London, Churchill and the Admiralty had reached the same conclusion and began to plan for Operation Dynamo—the evacuation of the BEF from France. Admiral Bertram Ramsey was appointed to take command of the planning for possible evacuation, which posed huge logistical problems not just on sea but on land as well. On May 20, he held his first planning meeting at Dover. Once on land the problems did not end. For example, the port of Dover had eight births for cross channel ferries, each of which would soon be used by up to three ships at once. Once off the ships the men needed to be moved away from the dock, fed and housed. Not surprising that when planning began, the best Ramsey hoped to achieve was to rescue 45,000 men over two days. On the east coast ships were being assembled in readiness for the evacuation order. In France, the BEF was retreating further toward the French port of Dunkirk. On May 24, Boulogne fell to the Germans and Calais was only just holding out. German tanks were now just 15 kms from Dunkirk. At this crucial juncture, Hitler ordered his tanks to stop ("Halt order") having apparently agreed with Gen von Rundstedt (Army Group A) that the armored divisions should be husbanded for the second phase of the campaign (Operation Red) thus allowing the infantry and Luftwaffe to tackle the Allied troops (Goring had reputedly boasted that his Luftwaffe could finish the task on its own). When Calais fell on May 26, Operation Dynamo was put into effect.

Due to war-time censorship and the desire to keep up the morale of the nation, the full extent of the unfolding "disaster" around Dunkirk was not publicized. However, the grave plight of the troops led King George VI to call for an unprecedented week of prayer. Throughout the country, people prayed on May 26 for a miraculous delivery. The archbishop of Canterbury led prayers "for our soldiers in dire peril in France." On May 26, the British and the French had both decided to form a beachhead around Dunkirk but for different reasons. While the British hoped to escape from the German trap, the French still hoped to fight on (this would later fuel the belief as far as the French were concerned that the British were ready to fight to the last Frenchman).

As the last of the BEF landed in England, a different kind of war was being waged. It was the propaganda battle and in Britain it would be disseminated largely through the Ministry of Information and it new minister, Duff Cooper (Lord Reith had just been replaced).

Even though Britain had suffered a catastrophic defeat, "Dunkirk" took on an immediate mythic resonance for the British people. It symbolized their brave and resourceful resistance to German military might. To that extent, Dunkirk had a profound inspirational effect, which helped Britain continue fighting even when her position seemed hopeless. Out of the feat of human salvage, the British forged a propaganda triumph.

It is important to set the myth that was to be created about Dunkirk into wider perspective. Churchill and Duff Cooper (and others in the government) were afraid that Dunkirk (a beaten and outmaneuvered army that had retreated chaotically, abandoned in some case by their officers) would lead to pessimism and defeatism in the public and set up public-survey schemes to test the popular mood. Those in authority, therefore, showed a misplaced lack of confidence in the British people. Grumblers were prosecuted for causing disaffection and discontent until Churchill put a stop to it. Duff Cooper sent round investigators to probe public opinion (dismissed by those investigated as "Cooper's Snoopers") and sought to rouse the nation by reciting Macaulay's poem on the Armada over the radio. British propaganda did not have a particularly persuasive start to World War II. That would change as a result of Dunkirk.

Manufacturing the Myth

Although Churchill had warned in the Commons that "wars are not won by evacuations," his own radio broadcasts (largely repeated from speeches given in the House) did much to catch the defiant mood of the people and express the spirit of the hour (interesting because he had *not* previously been rated highly as a radio speaker. His resonant voice and rotund phrases were out of keeping with the fashionable radio undertones—to coin a phrase by A.J.P. Taylor).

The newspapers were the first to pick up on the propaganda significance of the evacuation. On May 31, the *Daily Express* reported that tens of thousands of British troops were safely home already: "tired, dirty, hungry—they came back unbeatable!" The report was one of the first to pay tribute to the crews of the civilian ships: " the old tramp steamers, ships of all sorts and sizes, even barges in tow . . . whose crews went into the blast and hell on the other side."

On June 3, the *Daily Sketch* reported reassuringly, over a photograph headlined "The Navy's Here—with the Army" that four-fifths of the BEF had been saved. Interestingly, it wasn't until June 6 (i.e., after the evacuation had been completed) that the British newsreels began to trumpet the extraordinary achievements of the evacuation from Dunkirk. Here is an example of the first Pathé Gazette newsreel coverage dated June 6: "The Greatest Epic of the War."

The newsreel begins with "a curtain of darkness hangs over the coast of Britain." Like all the newsreels, it gives the impression of immediacy (which was their brief)—yet confirms that we know the outcome of the drama unfolding: "here in pictures is the triumph that turned a major military disaster into a miracle of deliverance." Interesting also that it refers to what we are dishing out: "and the enemy paid four folds for our loses" (this would be a major concern of the British people during the first 18 months of the war that was picked up by Mass Observation. "We know what we are taking and that we can take it—but what were we giving the Hun?"). There is also a rare hint of war realism at the end with the reference to the sacrifices and losses of the rear-guard forces that remained on the beaches. The newsreel ends with the invocation to look to the future, which was encapsulated in Churchill's famous speech "we shall never surrender."

Newspaper cartoonists, however, were quick to pick up on the role of ordinary citizens and the "everyday, matter-of-fact" aspect of the evacuation and the manner in which British people rallied in a defining moment of crisis. On June 5, Sidney (George) Strube in the *Daily Express* referred to this miraculous evacuation as "All in the days work." The captain of the little boat (*Saucy Jane*) is depicted in one scene ("Then") carrying holiday makers to and from his boat with seagulls overhead and in another ("Now") carrying a wounded (but fully equipped) British Tommy with the Luftwaffe lurking above.

So, British propaganda picked up on the theme of snatching (a sort) of victory out of the jaws of defeat, and almost immediately a myth began to develop that would help sustain the British war effort. One of the most important aspects was the galvanizing slogan of we live to fight another day. Again, British cartoonists were quick to pick on this theme. On June 8, 1940, David Low, in the *Evening Standard*, showed how the motley collection of little ships packed with evacuated soldiers had allowed the nation "To fight another day." Printed on opposite page was an editorial: "By a prodigious effort of bravery and resource, a rag-tag-and-bobtail fleet of any and every kind of craft that could float, assisted by the British Navy and Air Force, withdrew the surrounded B.E.F. from Dunkirk. Four-fifths of the troops were snatched from the trap. Hitler's first slip."[1] The little ships of Dunkirk not only connected with the established seafaring myths of the British, they also exemplified those qualities so beloved by the British—improvisation, amateurism, and individualism.

The myth is part of the national memory of World War II, which can be broken down into various "sub-myths" including those of evacuation (Dunkirk), the battle of Britain, and the Blitz. The myth of Dunkirk was created by people actively accepting an interpretation of events, often inspired by the media, which then provided a model that shaped actions in times of crisis. And following Dunkirk, Britain stood alone and in desperate trouble (another slogan taken up by the media when France was forced to sign an Armistice). When France collapsed, King George VI famously wrote to his mother: "Personally, I feel happier now that we have no allies to be polite to and pamper."[2] So Dunkirk allowed us to fight another day—but essentially alone. Mass Observation detected a sense of relief that Britain could now concentrate all effort on the *defense* of the home country and "standing alone" reflected a genuine patriotism, founded upon centuries of belief in the apartness of Britain (an island race). J. B. Priestley had alluded to this in his *Postscripts* radio broadcast of June 5: "Now that it is all over, and we can look back on it, doesn't it seem to you to have an inevitable air about it—as if we can turn a page in the history of Britain and seen a chapter headed 'Dunkirk'" (see Document 3). David Low captured this spirit in one of his most famous cartoons of the World War II. In "Very Well, Alone" (*Evening Standard*, June 18, 1940), Low summed up a common feeling of stoic resolution. Unlike many of Low's cartoons, there is no humor in the message. He sketches, instead, an angry-looking English soldier standing on the white cliffs of Dover, his arm outstretched toward France (which had just fallen) and his fist clenched at the oncoming Luftwaffe emerging from a looming black cloud. Low's cartoon captured the image of dogged resilience, the apotheosis of the bulldog spirit the British liked to project in times of adversity.

Winston Churchill also appealed to this mixture of patriotism, insularity, and xenophobia in his "We shall fight on the beaches . . . We shall never surrender" speech to the House of Commons on June 4 (extracts of which were later that evening broadcast on the BBC): "I have, myself, full confidence that if all do their duty, if nothing is neglected, and if the best arrangements are made, as they are being made, we shall prove ourselves once again able to defend our island homes, to ride out the storm of war, and to outlive the menace of tyranny, if necessary for years, if necessary *alone.*"

The heroism of the Dunkirk campaign and of the BEF had set a benchmark for the British people; the "Dunkirk spirit" or in this case the "Dunkirk mood" had become a shorthand for heroism and resilience. Bearing in mind the newsreels we have just seen and the point I made about the importance attached in British propaganda of presenting the united efforts of our armed forces combining to achieve this "miracle," I want to finish by showing a famous scene from *In Which We Serve*, Noel Coward's portrait of the Royal Navy and the most popular film in Britain in 1942. It includes a Dunkirk sequence. HMS Torrin's crew (with Coward at the helm) pick up survivors and take them to Dover where they disembark. Gradually a bedraggled company are called to order, their spirit restored and they march off in perfect time to the sounds of a band. Leading seaman "Shorty" Blake (John Mills) makes the only comment: "If I wasn't so tired, I'd give 'em a cheer and no mistake." It is an extraordinary poignant scene that somehow freezes the national myth of Dunkirk and echoes the headline of the *Daily Mirror* on June 3, which proclaimed: "And still they come back—Gort's unbreakables!"

Notes

1. *Evening Standard*, June 8, 1940.
2. Quoted in L. Thompson, *1940: Year of Legend, Year of History* (London: Collins, 1966), 132.

Chapter 7

Careless Talk

During the first year of the war, the British government was deeply concerned to prevent information reaching the enemy, a fear influenced by the widespread talk in the media about the alleged operations of Nazi Fifth Columns in countries invaded by Germany. The campaign, which quickly became referred to as "careless talk," started with a simple but stark warning on posters and leaflets: "Do not discuss anything which might be of national importance. The consequences of any such indiscretion may be the loss of many lives."

The Ministry of Information (MOI) was responsible for distributing 2½ million posters and leaflets to offices, shops, public houses, and so on. Careless talk propaganda discouraged talking about sensitive material where it could be overheard by spies, showing either an Axis eavesdropper or depicting a death caused by such information leaking. Following the initial government warning that established the anti-gossip campaign, an equally uninspiring and short-lived "Silent Column" campaign, which Winston Churchill had requested, followed in July 1940 to deal with rumors. The MOI's newspaper advertisements urged the population to "Join Britain's Silent Column":

> You will wear no uniform, you will not spend nights on lonely duty. Your only weapons will be your commonsense, your ears and your tongue . . . The country asks you to join the Silent Colum—the great body of sensible people who know when not to talk and who will, in the event of an invasion, stop the rumours that lead to confusion . . . It will not be easy—to be a loyal member of the Silent Column you'll need a great deal of self-control and courage to speak up in order to keep dangerous speech down. . . . Most people talk dangerously without realizing that they are doing so. Tactfully point out what they are saying should be left unsaid. If somebody starts talking rumour take out an old envelope and start writing down what they are saying.

Not surprisingly, given its dull and lecturing tone (to the extent that an even "old" envelope is instructed), the Silent Column did not work, as Harold Nicholson (at the time working in the MOI) noted in his diary in July 1940: "There is no doubt our anti-rumour campaign has been a ghastly failure . . . Partly because our silence campaign and the prosecutions for gossip which have taken place in the country have caused justified irritation. And partly because the country is in a bad state of nerves during this lull before the storm." Churchill duly axed the campaign.

A lighter touch was required and it came in the form of Cyril Kenneth Bird, a well-known cartoonist and editor of the magazine *Punch*, when war broke out. Bird worked under the name "Fougasse" and he persuaded the MOI to use humor for wartime propaganda and offered his services for free. He believed the sharing of a joke enabled a poster to persuade without causing resentment by appearing to preach. He deliberately set out to tackle the problem of public apathy in the face of an onslaught of posters by using an arresting sense of humor, together with a totally individual simplified technique, which the eye could absorb at a glance. He isolated his designs from other distractions by a gulf of white space enclosed in a neat red border.

Fougasse designed a series of eight posters for the Careless Talk Cost Lives campaign. One showed two women—Hitler and a bemedaled Göring sitting behind them—with one saying to the other, "You never know who's listening!" Fougasse also drew a man and woman seated at the dinner table, one saying to the other: "Of course there's no harm in your knowing!," an eager Hitler crouching under the table with his notebook. Some 2.5 million copies of these posters were printed and brought an element of humor into the government's until then rather earnest propaganda. They were produced in a variety of formats both for indoor and outdoor display and proved so popular that they were even reproduced on textiles.

Document 8 is a silk handkerchief designed by "Fougasse" for the Ministry of Information's careless Talk Cost Lives' campaign. It consists of five of his most popular posters and bears testimony to the popularity of his work with wartime British audiences.

Document 8

"YOU NEVER KNOW WHO'S LISTENING": A SILK HANDKERCHIEF DESIGNED BY "FOUGASSE" (CYRIL KENNETH BIRD) FOR THE MINISTRY OF INFORMATION'S "CARELESS TALK COST LIVES" CAMPAIGN (CIRCA 1942)

Document

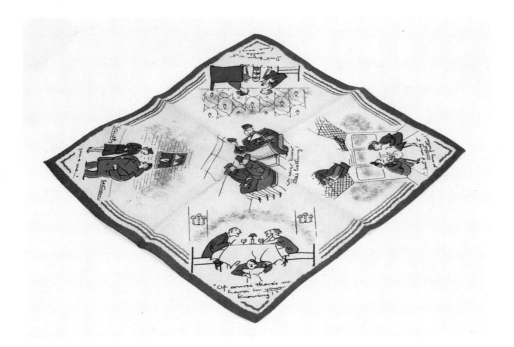

Source: Imperial War Museum (EPH 3034), © IWM.

Analysis

Careless Talk campaigns featured in every country's propaganda. Generally they attempted to arouse a sense of horror at the results of indiscretion. In America, one of the best examples of this approach is John Atherton's poster "A carless word . . . another cross" showing a dead soldier's helmet dangling from a homemade cross. In 1943, the RMVP produced a brilliant poster "The Enemy Overhears!" (*Feind hört mit!*) with a menacing shadow intended to represent a foreign spy, eavesdropping on a conversation between a German sailor and his girlfriend. In Britain, Abram Games took this approach a stage further by visually linking the careless talker and his victims. "Your Talk May Kill Your Comrades" (1942) shows how what comes out of the mouth of a serviceman leads directly to a bullet in the back for three comrades. Other British wartime slogans on this theme included "Keep It Under Your Hat," "Be

Like Dad, Keep Mum," and "Keep Mum She's Not So Dumb!" The latter, by Gerald Lacoste (1940) depicts a glamorous blond vamp reclining, surrounded by indiscreet officers from each branch of the armed forces. It is implied that the officers are talking military secrets, on the (wrongful) assumption that the woman is only a "dumb blonde" and so will not pass these secrets onto the enemy. Some of these posters aroused criticism among feminists, including Dame Edith Summerskill.

POTATO PETE'S RECIPE BOOK (GB, 1941)

Document

SCALLOPED POTATOES

1 lb. potatoes   1 tablespoon flour
$\frac{1}{2}$ pint milk or half milk
A few breadcrumbs
Half vegetable stock
Salt and pepper to taste
Chopped parsley, sliced spring onion, or
    chopped celery to taste

Method — Scrub and scrape the potatoes, then cut them into fairly thin slices. Arrange the layers in a pie-dish or casserole, sprinkling each layer with seasoned flour. Layer with a little chopped parsley and the minced celery or onion. Pour in the milk, sprinkle the top with breadcrumbs and bake in a moderate oven for about one hour, or cook in a frying pan covered with a plate for $\frac{1}{2}$ to $\frac{3}{4}$ hour over low heat.

Source: Imperial War Museum (LBY K.14/961.1 and LBY K. 03/2139), © IWM.

Analysis

Total war in the 20th century provided a major spur for propaganda. During World War II, we witness governments employing propaganda for a wide range of objectives. While a stress on people's obligations toward their country in the "Your country needs you" spirit was appropriate in times of war, governments were becoming increasingly conscious—partly as a result of the sacrifices made during these wars—of their responsibility toward their own citizens. In World War II, propaganda came to have an important instructional role in conveying public information on issues such as health and hygiene. Today, the promotion of public health has become a staple subject of propaganda, from governmental and nongovernmental organizations alike, throughout the world. Public health campaigns are sometimes known as "soft" propaganda—a gentler way of spreading ideas or customs.

In World War II, health campaigns figured even more prominently in official propaganda. The wartime emergency meant that citizens had to be physically fit in order to fight, work in industry, cope with air raids, and endure hardship caused by food and other shortages. In Britain, adequate food supplies were recognized as a key factor in the maintenance of morale. The British government mobilized a number of ministries to explain official policy and to stress the importance of good health for the successful conclusion of the war effort. The Ministry of Food was thus one of the largest spenders on publicity, issuing a constant flow of leaflets and press advertisements, as well as short films explaining the rationing system and providing wartime recipes and ways of making limited supplies last longer.

The Ministry of Agriculture was responsible for increasing the amount of land under cultivation in order to grow more vegetables. One of the most famous slogans of the war was "Dig for Victory." Britain's Home Front was encouraged to transform private gardens into mini-allotments. It was believed, quite rightly, that this would not only provide essential crops for families and neighborhoods but would help the war effort by freeing up valuable space for war materials (rather than food imports) on the merchant shipping convoys. Over 10 million instructional leaflets were distributed to the British people. The Kitchen Front radio broadcasts were concerned with using food efficiently, as well as with making use of what was readily available to mitigate shortages. In addition to the circulation of familiar Ministry of Agriculture "food flashes," literature and poster displays, anthems were also introduced, including one under the slogan "Dig for Victory":

Dig! Dig! Dig!
And your muscles will grow big.
Keep on pushing the spade.
Don't mind the worms.
Just ignore their squirms
And when your back aches laugh with glee.
And keep on diggin'.
Till we give our foes a Wiggin' Dig!
Dig! Dig! to Victory

Carrots were one vegetable in plentiful supply, and as a result widely became a substitute for the more scarce commodities. To improve their blandness, people were encouraged to "enjoy" the healthy carrot in different ways by the introduction of such characters as "Doctor Carrot." The Ministry of Agriculture suggested such culinary delights as curried carrot, carrot jam, and a homemade drink called Carrolade (made from the juices of carrots and swede).

Potato Pete was another character introduced to encourage the population to eat homegrown vegetables. As with the Dig for Victory theme, Potato Pete also had his own song amplifying the message. With vocals by Betty Driver (later Betty Williams in the television soap opera "Coronation Street"), the recording was a great success and did a tremendous amount of good in getting the message across:

> Here's the man who ploughs the fields.
> Here's the girl who lifts up the yield.
> Here's the man who deals with the clamp,
> So that millions of jaws can chew and champ.
> That's the story and here's the star,
> Potato Pete—Eat up, ta ta!

Potato Pete recipe books gave women suggestions and advice on how best to serve potatoes at mealtimes. For example, "scrubbing instead of peeling" was recommended, thus avoiding unnecessary wastage. Even traditional nursery rhymes were adapted to give a Potato Pete theme.

The propaganda campaign was successful. It was estimated that over 1,400,000 people acquired mini-allotments by turning lawns and flower beds into vegetable gardens. By 1943, over a million tons of vegetables were being grown in gardens and allotments. People were encouraged to keep chickens, and some kept rabbits and goats. Pigs were especially popular because they could be fed on kitchen waste. As the Minister of Food during this period, Lord Woolton was responsible for explaining the benefits of rationing to the British public and educating them into better eating habits. Later in the war, with plentiful vegetables being produced as a result of the success of the Dig for Victory campaign, some were used as the ingredients for the legendary Woolton Pie, a vegetable pie made from potatoes, parsnips, and herbs. Unsurprisingly, it was a dish that never really took off with the British public. The Potato Pete recipe book is an excellent example of how propaganda invaded the "everyday" experiences of ordinary citizens fighting total war.

Document 10

BOO-BOO BRINGS DOWN AN ENEMY AIRPLANE (1943)

Document

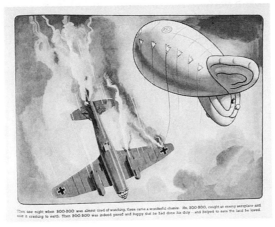

Source: The Welch Collection.

Analysis

The notion of civil responsibility extended to children as well. As far as good health was concerned, the Ministry of Health targeted children with a series of posters that encouraged parents and children (milkman, "Please leave extra milk for me") to order an extra pint of milk for their children: "The Essential Food for Growing Children." Moreover, a number of illustrated books for young children were produced that acknowledged the war and the manner in which the British community pulled together in the war effort (e.g., *Wimpy the Wellington*, 1942).[1] The bulbous, protective shape of the barrage balloon proved particularly popular. In *Boo-Boo the Barrage Balloon* (1943), full-page colored pictures have a simple narrative running beneath. Boo-Boo, a brave and patriotic barrage balloon (the invention of Professors Flip, Flop, and Pumblechook), married Belinda and they produce twin baby barrage balloons (Betty and Basil). Together, they guard the skies of Britain. Having caught an enemy aircraft and sent it crashing to earth, the text delivers the propaganda message of the importance of civil responsibility and pride: "Then Boo-Boo was indeed proud and happy that he had done his duty—and helped to save the land he loved." Boo-Boo was awarded a medal for his bravery, but interestingly, the book ends by emphasizing the role to be played by the proud twins, Betty and Basil: "Of course, nothing would satisfy the twins but that Boo-Boo should come down to earth and teach them to be good barrage balloons so that they could grow like Daddy, and perhaps some day win a medal. And splendid pupils they were, too!"

Note

1. "Wimpy" was a Wellington bomber that "has been Right Round the World, AND has rescued a Very Famous American General, AND has a big Gold Bomb on his nose signed by the President of the United States of America." The anthropomorphizing of the bomber, complete with waistcoat button and eyes in the engine nacelles, was undertaken by the political cartoonist of the *Daily Mirror*, Philip Zec. *Wimpy the Wellington* (London: Frederick Miller, 1942), 30. See, K Agnew and G. Fox, *Children at War* (London: Continuum, 2001), 23–24.

Chapter 8
Nazi Anti-British and Anti-Bolshevik Propaganda

Document 11
A NAZI LEAFLET DURING THE BATTLE OF BRITAIN (1941)

Document

WANTED

FOR INCITEMENT TO
MURDER

Source: Imperial War Museum (K AERIAL 3/3591). © IWM.

Analysis

Anti-Jewish and anti-Bolshevik motifs were central to the Nazi *Weltanschauung* ("worldview"). The Nazi movement had developed and finally emerged from a struggle in which communists together with the Jews formed the main target of Nazi violence and invective. Indeed, by claiming a Marxist-inspired Jewish-Bolshevik conspiracy, Nazi propaganda was able, at times, to fuse these two enemies into one. However, for a brief period following the defeat of France in 1940, German propagandists switched to targeting the British. Once Britain had declared war on Germany in September 1939, it became a distinctive enemy and object of hatred in Nazi propaganda. Throughout the early part of the summer of 1940, as the struggle for control of the skies above Britain took place, anti-British propaganda reached a new crescendo, claiming that it was only a matter of time before Britain's fate was sealed. Propaganda emphasized British hypocrisy and "plutocracy."

Prime Minister Winston Churchill, in particular, was targeted and mercilessly lampooned. One famous poster in Nazi Germany depicted him as an American-style gangster with the text *Heckenschützen* ("The Sniper"), brandishing a machine gun. Goebbels used the same image for leaflets dropped over the United Kingdom during the Battle of Britain with the text in English "WANTED," and at the bottom, "for incitement to MURDER." The reverse of the leaflet is all text: it refers to Churchill as a "gangster" responsible for the hardships suffered by ordinary citizens during the bombing of British cities. The SD Reports (of the *Sicherheitsdienst*, secret police) suggested that German hatred of Britain, incited by incessant propaganda, was now widespread.

Document 12

NAZI ANTI-BRITISH POSTCARD (1942)

Document

Source: The Welch Collection.

Analysis

During the same period, the Nazis produced a postcard showing a beleaguered Churchill-like admiral aboard the ship of Britain, surrounded by mines and about to swallow a German bomb. The text is a play on words, but translates as "For you things are going to get really rotten . . . We're going to use a Stuka to shut your big mouth!" This card was sent from Kassel in 1942, a city that, ironically, would be largely destroyed by Allied bombs.

After the failure to invade Britain in 1940, with Göring's Luftwaffe decisively checked in the Battle of Britain, Hitler switched his attack and invaded the Soviet Union on June 22, 1941. The anti-Bolshevik motif was central to the Nazi *Weltanschauung* ("worldview"). The movement had created an environment in which Communists, together with Jews, formed the main target of Nazi propaganda and violence. Russia figured not only as the center of world Communism but also as the repository of international Jewry.

Document 13

GERMAN ANTI-BOLSHEVIK POSTER: "EUROPE'S VICTORY IS YOUR PROSPERITY" (1942)

Document

Analysis

The anti-Bolshevik poster proclaims that Germany has destroyed Great Britain (depicted as one graveyard, with Churchill's grave symbolically prominent), and shows how the mailed fist of Germany is turning its attention to the East—threatening a knock-out blow for Stalin and the Soviet Union. The justification in the poster for the invasion of the USSR (in violation of the Nazi-Soviet Nonaggression Pact, 1939) is security (baby in a cradle) and prosperity (living space for Germans).

In propaganda terms the messages employed in these documents would return to haunt the Nazi leadership when, in 1943, an undefeated RAF began to bomb German cities.

Chapter 9
In Defense of Mother Russia

A FILM POSTER FOR THE FILM, *ALEXANDER NEVSKY* (1938–1941)

Document

Analysis

Soviet propaganda was determined by the Council of People's Commissars and the Political Bureau of the All Union Communist Party. It was supervised by the Directorate of Propaganda and Agitation of the Central Committee under A. S. Shcherbakov and administered by the newly established Soviet Information Bureau. These propaganda organizations together with Soviet political leadership were caught by surprise when the Germans invaded in June 1941. Only a week before, the Soviet news agency Tass had dismissed German troop movements in the East as "nothing but clumsy propaganda by forces hostile to the USSR and Germany and interested in an extension of the war."[1] The rapid German advance following the invasion of June 22, 1941 ("Operation Barbarossa"), together with the ease with which demoralized Russian troops capitulated (there were 5 million Russian prisoners of war by the end of 1941), suggested that a great deal had to done to restore morale.

Stalin immediately called for a "Great Patriotic Struggle" and mobilized the Soviet media for total war. In his "Holy Russia" speech of November 6, 1941, the 24th anniversary of the revolution, he stoked national pride by recalling great Russian generals of the past and associating them with towering cultural figures such as Pushkin, Tolstoy, Chekhov, and Tchaikovsky. Stalin's frequent references to Alexander Nevsky and Suvorov made the nation conscious of the link between the Russian past and present. To this end, one of the first propaganda initiatives was to rerelease the anti-German film, *Alexander Nevsky*.

In 1938, when Nazi foreign policy was increasingly expansionist, the great Russian film director, Sergei Eisenstein, produced the historical film epic *Alexander Nevsky*. Nevsky was conceived as a work of propaganda that would strengthen the resolve of all those in the USSR who were opposing Fascism. The film was an allegory, a projection of present events onto the past, an appeal to the example offered by Russian history. The story of this prince of Novgorod's legendary victory in 1242 over the Teutonic Knights, who were rampaging through what was now Russian territory (today in Estonia), clearly implied that Germans could not be relied upon to uphold peace treaties. The film was intended to arouse patriotic sentiment against the Nazi threat by emphasizing the despicable nature of the enemy, and Nevsky symbolized the spirit of Russia and its historical resistance to foreign invaders. When Soviet policy changed abruptly in August 1939, with the Nazi-Soviet Nonaggression Pact, Stalin banned the film; but it was rereleased in 1941 after the Nazi invasion.

In *Alexander Nevsky*, the conventional meanings of light and dark are inverted. Eisenstein consciously allowed the lighter shades to represent the enemy and the darker ones the heroes (juxtapositions that are heightened by Sergei Prokofiev's dramatic score). The cunning high priest of the Teutonic order sports an emblem similar to a swastika on his collar and helmet. The Germans are depicted as ruthless and heartless, and they commit numerous atrocities. In an extraordinarily brutal scene, the Teutonic Knights, in full military regalia with their monstrous helmets, murder innocent children by callously throwing them into a fire. The Germans are faceless, often hooded and frequently shot in profile, with cruel, animal-like features. One scene, following the sacking of the city of Pskov, shows fleeing refugees and wounded soldiers calling for vengeance. Tension mounts as stories of the German atrocities are recounted:

Soldier: If they catch you with a sword, they beat you for having it! If they catch you with bread, they beat you for the bread! They've tortured mothers and wives for their sons and husbands.

Crowd: The German is a beast! We know the Germans!

The Russian victory is ultimately confirmed by a one-to-one struggle between Alexander Nevsky and the Master of the Teutonic Order. The German forces gather around their war horn, and the ice covering Lake Peipus, on which the battle took place, cracks beneath them. Like the forces of Napoleon and, in due course, those of Hitler, they fall victim to the Russian winter. At the end of the film, Alexander addresses his army and his people with the warning: "Let people come to us as guests without fear. But he who comes with sword shall perish . . . Arise people of Russia. To glorious battle, mortal battle! Arise, men of freedom. For our fair land!"

Not only was Alexander to symbolize the spirit of Russia and its resistance to invaders, but contemporary audiences would also have made the obvious "connections" in the light of Stalin's "personality cult." Equally obvious was the parallel with the USSR's current situation following the Nazi invasion. *Alexander Nevsky* proved extremely popular with Russian cinema audiences and played an important part in laying the ground for the wartime leadership cult of Stalin, with its mixture of ideology and patriotism. Later in the war, Stalin would invoke the memory of Alexander Nevsky to inspire the Russian people in their struggle against Nazi Germany. Images of Nevsky appeared on a number of Soviet posters with quotations attributed to Stalin such as "Our cause is just! Fight to the death! 'Let the courage of our great ancestors inspire you.'" So powerful was the role the film played in strengthening the Soviet resistance that Stalin instituted a new battle honor: the Order of Alexander Nevsky.

In the 1930s, totalitarian regimes had recognized the importance of film as a powerful propaganda tool. In Italy and in Germany, the cinema had been quickly utilized by Mussolini and Hitler to disseminate Fascist and Nazi ideology. In the USSR, Lenin had declared that "for us the cinema is the most important of all the arts." For totalitarian police states, World War II posed few difficulties as constraints on artistic and commercial license and strict censorship had been intrinsic elements in their *Filmpolitik* and required little adjustment to wartime exigencies. Feature films, documentaries, and newsreels were extensively used to provide a justification for war and a partial and ideological view of wartime developments.

For the democracies, on the other hand, wartime restraint posed real strains between the demands of government fighting "total war" and the needs of a commercial cinema industry delivering entertainment for profit to a mass audience. In Great Britain, for example, the biggest difficulty facing the MOI would be that of news management. How could a government in a nation that prided itself on freedom of speech and information become an overbearing censor, particularly when it chose to fight in the name of freedom. The MOI was initially slow to act in the case of film propaganda. The first propaganda film of the war, *The Lion Has Wings* (1939), was produced independently of the MOI by Alexander Korda. But by 1940, the MOI had drawn up a policy for film propaganda and it had established the Crown Film Unit to produce short information and documentary films. These "drama-documentaries" showed ordinary people carrying out their wartime jobs but placed them within a genuine dramatic framework. Humphrey Jennings made a film during the blitz about London's firemen *Fires Were Started* (1943); Harry Watt showed how a bomber station prepared for a raid and the men who carried it out in *Target for Tonight* (1941) and Pat Jackson paid tribute to the men of the Merchant Navy in *Western Approaches* (1944).

The MOI wanted the British film industry to help it promote three main themes: why we fight, how we fight and the sacrifices necessary to achieve victory. In order to achieve these objectives, it recognized (eventually) that "for the film to be good propaganda, it must also be good entertainment." Going to the cinema remained a normal part of people's life and by far the most popular form of entertainment, particularly for the working classes. In 1939, 19 million people went to the cinema in Britain every week and by 1945 the figure had risen to 30 million—half the population. People went to the cinema to see the main feature, and it was there that propaganda, if skillfully handled, could be most effectively insinuated, while the audience was relaxed and thus off its guard. By the end of the war, despite the fact that 80 percent of films seen weekly were American, British films were enjoying an unprecedented degree of popularity and success. The war has transformed the British cinema.[2]

Once America entered the war in December 1941, Hollywood was swift to mobilize its resources behind the war effort. On December 17, 1941, 10 days after Pearl Harbor, President Roosevelt appointed Lowell Mellett—an ardent New Dealer and Roosevelt aide who was a former editor of Scripps-Howard's *Washington Daily News*—to serve as coordinator of government films, acting as a liaison between the government and the motion picture industry, and advising Hollywood in its support of the war effort. To this end, he was ably supported by deputy chief, Nelson Paynter. Roosevelt had stated, "The motion picture industry could be the most powerful instrument of propaganda in the world, whether it tries to be or not."[3] The studios quickly copyrighted crude, topical movie titles, such as *The War against Mrs. Hadley* (1942), *Saboteur* (1942), *Flying Tigers* (1942), and *V for Victory* (1941). Warner Brothers ordered a hasty rewrite of *Across the Pacific* (1942), which involved a Japanese plot to blow up Pearl Harbor, changing the setting to the Panama Canal.

Once the Office of War Information (OWI) had been set up in June 1942, Mellet's office became the Bureau of Motion Pictures (BMP) and eventually issued a manual to Hollywood listing the kind of themes that would serve the national effort. The other agency within the OWI dealing with films was the Office of Censorship, which oversaw film exports. Classified as "an essential war industry," Roosevelt insisted: "I want no restrictions place thereon which will impair the usefulness of the film other than those very necessary restrictions which the dictates of safety make imperative." Taking its lead from the president, the OWI and the BMP preferred to convert Hollywood, not censor it. Poynter played a prominent role here in attempting to win over the powerful Hollywood studios that remained wary of incremental government censorship and diktats.

The OWI hoped that the studios would make fewer combat films and more serious films dramatizing the issues of the war, notably the Four Freedoms (see Document 2). Like the MOI in Britain, the OWI hoped to capitalize on the innate ingenuity of the commercial film industry and the susceptibility of cinema audiences to be influenced by artfully constructed entertainment films imbued with subtle propaganda messages. As OWI's director Elmer Davis put it, "The easiest way to inject a propaganda idea into most people's minds is to let it go in through the medium of an entertainment picture when they do not realize that they are being propagandized."[4] In the summer of 1942, following exchanges with Hollywood studios, BMP believed that the movie industry needed some sort of steer and so assembled their suggestions in the "Government Information Manual for the Motion Picture Industry."

Document 15

GOVERNMENT INFORMATION MANUAL FOR THE MOTION PICTURE INDUSTRY (SECTIONS I-VI, USA, 1942)

Document

Introduction

[. . .]

The Government Information Program is predicated on the following basic premises:

1. The overwhelming majority of the people are behind the government in its war program but they do not have adequate knowledge and understanding of this program. In the United States we are not for "blind followers." Unless the public adequately understands the war program, a few military reverses can shatter the high morale of the American people. Unless they adequately understand the magnitude of the program, the people will not willingly make the additional sacrifices that they shall be called upon to make in the prosecution of total war and total victory.

    The Government of the United States has an unwavering faith in the sincerity of purpose and integrity of the American people. The American people, on the whole, are not susceptible to The Strategy of Lies. They prefer truth as the vehicle for understanding. The government believes that truth in the end is the only medium to bring about the proper understanding of democracy, the one important ingredient that can help make democracy work. Axis propagandists have failed. They have not told the truth, and their peoples are now beginning to see through this sham. If we are to keep faith with the American people, we must not resort to any devious information tactics. We must meet lies with a frontal attack—with the weapon of truth.

2. We believe that mass opinion is intelligent and will support an intelligent program—*if informed*. The people will support a program of decency and integrity, idealism and enlightened selfishness—*if adequately informed*.

3. We believe that support of Fascism can be marshaled only from the ignorant, the frustrated and the poverty-stricken, in some measure backed by reactionary men of wealth. We must keep these groups in mind constantly and try to overcome their ignorance, their frustration and their want.

Section 1. The Issues: Why We Fight

What Kind of Peace Will Follow Victory?

If we are to win this war, Americans must be ready to sacrifice comforts, necessities, and life itself. Public opinion polls indicate that some confusion still exists as to the issues for which this war is being fought. Unless every American clearly understands how much he has at stake, the nations cannot gear itself to the all-out effort necessary for victory.

The motion picture should be the best medium for bringing to life the democratic idea. We practical-minded Americans can easily grasp such tangible programs as sugar-rationing or pooling of cars to save rubber. It is a challenge to the ingenuity of Hollywood to make equally real the democratic values which we take for granted.

What Are We Fighting For?

1. *We are fighting for survival as a nation.* Some people do not realize that the actual existence of this nation as a politically independent state depends on winning the war.

2. *We are fighting for freedom and against slavery.* For
    a. Freedom of speech
    b. Freedom of religion
    c. Freedom from want
    d. Freedom from fear.

    We must make the Four Freedoms live and breathe. They must not become mere trademarks. Each individual must know how these Four Freedoms affect his individual life, his everyday affairs. Few of our people have any real grasp of what life would mean to them as individuals if the Axis were to win.

    The realization must be driven home that we cannot enjoy the Four Freedoms exclusively. They must be established on a world-wide basis—yes, even in Germany, Italy, and Japan—or they will always be in jeopardy in America.

3. *We are fighting for a New World.* We are fighting for a more decent world—a world free from force and militarism. We are fighting not only to maintain for ourselves the gains we have made in the past, but also for the right to build a new and better life "for all people and for future generations." We are fighting for democracy among nations as among individuals, for a world community dedicated to the free flow of trade, ideas, and culture.

Source: Washington National Records Centre, Maryland, OWI Files Box 15.

Analysis

Document 15 is an extract from the manual and is a key document in understanding the relationship between film and propaganda during the war. According to the film historians, Clayton Koppes and Gregory Black, "the manual represents a comprehensive statement of OWI's vision of America, the war and the world."[5] The manual constituted 42 pages and was issued in loose leaf so that updates from the OWI/BMP could be incorporated whenever necessary. The bureau's war aims were imbued with Vice President Henry Wallace's *Century of the Common Man* (1943), the bible of liberals and left-liberals at war. The BMP manual described the global conflict as a "people's war" between freedom and fascism. The enemy was not the German, Italian, or Japanese people but the ruling elites and their ideologies. The war was a struggle between light and darkness (a theme that Frank Capra took up in his *Why We Fight* film documentaries, especially *Prelude to War*—see Document 4). America was fighting for the Four Freedoms worldwide and as such an Allied victory promised the world a New Deal, which would combine a regulated capitalism with an extension of social welfare programs; America would abandon isolationism to participate in a system of collective security.

OWI/BMP maintained that the studios could make any films they wanted and distribute them in the United States, so long as they were not treasonable. However, because film was so important to the war effort, it asked filmmakers to consider seven key questions:

1. Will this picture help win the war?

2. What war information problem does it seek to clarify, dramatize, or interpret?

3. If it is an "escape" picture. Will it harm the war effort by creating a false picture of America, her allies, or the world we live in?

4. Does it merely use the war as the basis for a profitable picture, contributing nothing of real significance to the war effort and possibly lessening the effect of other pictures of more importance?

5. Does it contribute something new to our understanding of the world conflict and the various forces involved, or has the subject already been adequately covered?

6. When the picture reaches its maximum circulation on the screen, will it reflect condition as they are and fill a need current at that time, or will it be outdated?

7. Does the picture tell the truth or will the young people of today have reason to say they were misled by propaganda.[6]

The OWI manual, which would be augmented by numerous "revisions," constituted a political and ideological blueprint for the Hollywood studios, without being too prescriptive that it would undermine the industry's profits. The cinema was, after all, a highly lucrative industry for America with a global reach. Of the seven "directives" the most important was arguably: "Will this picture help win the war?" Question 4 also warns Hollywood that the war should not be exploited for profit if such films contributed "nothing of real significance to the war effort and possibly lessening the effect of other pictures of more importance." However, the most revealing is point 7, which refers to "truth," "being misled," and "propaganda." This was clearly a reference to the experiences of World War I and the postwar reaction in America that the nation had been misled by "official" propaganda.[7]

Within the broader guidelines, six themes were identified as requiring priority (see Document 15): (1) to explain why the Americans were fighting; (2) the nature of our adversary; (3) to portray the United Nations and their peoples; (4) to encourage work and production; (5) to boost morale on the home front; and (6) to depict the heroics of the armed forces. These are broad themes and they were applied to American society in general, not specifically to Hollywood. For example, under "The Issues. Why We Fight," the manual called for two aspects to be dramatized: first, "We must emphasise that this is a people's war, that we must hang together or we shall all hang separately" and second, "We must emphasise the American heritage, the historical development that has made us what we are. What is the American way of life? It is a 1942 version of 1776."

Though jealously protective of its independence, Hollywood duly obliged by producing films about the "people's war," such as *Mrs. Minerva* (1942) (popular in the United States but mocked in Britain due to its rose-tinted Hollywood view of the Blitz), and about heroic resistance in Norway and France, such as *Joan of Paris* (1942) and *Edge of Darkness* (1943). The heroism and suffering of America's allies were also covered such as *Song of Russia* (1943), *Mission to Moscow* (1943),[8] *China* (1943), and *China Sky* (1945). Controversial domestic issues such as the role of Afro-American and anti-Semitism were also dealt with in *The Negro Soldier* (1944) and *Mr. Skeffington* (1943), albeit on a superficial level. Off the screen, leading actors and actresses led recruitment and bond drives and entertained the troops. Leading directors like Frank Capra, John Ford, and John Huston enlisted and made documentaries to explain, "why we fight" and to offer civilians an idea of what actual combat looked like. In less than a year, 12 percent of all film industry employees entered the armed forces, including Clark Gable, Henry Fonda, and Jimmy Stewart. By the war's end, one-quarter of Hollywood's male employees were in uniform.

Throughout the war, the BMP insisted that its job was to advise, not to censor. Indeed, the bureau could not bar production and exhibition of pictures it disapproved. But the OWI in fact had considerable power. As a government agency in wartime, it had to be taken very seriously; a recalcitrant studio risked accusations of not doing its bit for the war effort. Moreover, the Office of Censorship's control of export licenses gave the government economic leverage that the studios took seriously. Since its recommendations carried weight with the Office of Censorship, the OWI had more than patriotic persuasion at its command. The BMP was right to consider that every film enhanced or diminished the national reputation abroad. The manual that was issued to the film studios was judicious and recognized the unique qualities of the commercial film industry. Following the British lead, the Americans developed their "strategy of truth" as a fundamental principle of their propaganda, although OWI was prepared to manipulate cinema images in ways imperceptible to the public. In *its* turn, Hollywood responded in kind and produced some of the most stirring motion pictures and documentaries, which made a major contribution to the American war effort.

Notes

1. Quoted in Taylor, *Munitions of the Mind*, 235.

2. For a detailed analysis of the British cinema at war see, J. Chapman, *The British at War. Cinema, State and Propaganda, 1939–1945* (London: I.B. Tauris, 2000).

3. Cited in P. Taylor, *Munitions of the Mind. A History of Propaganda from the Ancient World to the Present Day* (Manchester: Manchester University Press, 1995), 229.

4. Quoted in C.R. Koppes and G.D. Black, *Hollywood Goes to War. How Politics, Profits and Propaganda Shaped World War II Movies* (Oakland: University of California Press, 1990), 64.

5. Koppes and Black, *Hollywood Goes to War*, 65. This work remains a key reference tool on the topic.

6. Ibid., 66.

7. Critics claimed that the United States has been duped into becoming involved on the Allied side, particularly by secret British propaganda emanating from Wellington House. This was seized upon by isolationist elements in American politics who now argued for noninvolvement in European affairs and for Americans to be on their guard against misleading and devious foreign propaganda.

8. The flexibility of the manual is illustrated by the case of *Mission to Moscow* (1943). The film violates the vast majority of the guidelines, was more notorious than any other Hollywood wartime feature film, yet was praised by the OWI censor, who thought it was terrific and just what was needed. See, D. Culbert (ed.), *Mission to Moscow* (Madison: University of Wisconsin Press, 1980).

Chapter 10

Mobilizing for Total War: The Witting and Unwitting Testimony

Document 16

JOSEPH GOEBBELS AND THE TOTAL WAR CAMPAIGN (1943)

Document

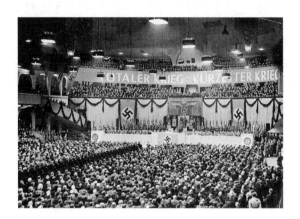

Source: Bundesarchiv Bild 183-J05235. German Federal Archive.

Analysis

When the war came, Hitler's astonishing run of *Blitzkrieg* victories, culminating in the fall of France, confirmed Goebbels's presentation of Hitler as a military genius who even confounded his own generals. When the war started to turn against Hitler in the winter of 1941–1942, it would take some time before military reverses had any noticeable effect on his popularity. However, following the catastrophe of Stalingrad, a defeat for which Hitler was held responsible, his popularity began to decline. Until Stalingrad, Hitler had been largely exempted from criticisms people had of the regime.

The impact of Stalingrad on the morale of the German people cannot be overestimated. It affected their attitude toward the war and created a crisis of confidence in the regime amongst broad sections of the population. Following Hitler's refusal to speak to the nation, graffiti appeared on walls attacking Hitler as "the Stalingrad Murderer." Hitherto, Nazi propaganda had always tried to give the impression that the Third Reich was waging one war with an unbending consistency. With its armies now on the defensive on three fronts, it was obvious that they were in fact fighting several wars and sometimes with contradictory objectives. The capture of the Sixth Army at Stalingrad did, however, bring Goebbels back into the forefront of German politics, and he, of course, did his best to give meaning to the catastrophe. In an attempt to sustain the myth of the heroic sacrifice of the Sixth Army, he claimed that their "heroic epic" was not in vain since it had served as the "bulwark of the historic European mission" in the fight against Bolshevism.

Stalingrad marked a turning point in Nazi war propaganda as it allowed Goebbels finally to implement his drive for the total mobilization of all Germany's human resources for the war effort. The fate of the Sixth Army gave impetus to the radical ideas he has been proposing for some time—the proclamation of "total war." Goebbels was one of the few Nazi leaders who had realized as early as 1942 that final victory could only be achieved by a full mobilization of German resources, which would incorporate every citizen. The propaganda minister envisaged a radical departure from the measures that other leaders like Martin Bormann had established for civil defense. For Goebbels, success could only be achieved by the complete mobilization of the home front in order that Germany should become one fighting body, united under a powerful leader. This entailed shifting propaganda strategy from the optimistic, almost arrogant claims of the previous three years. In particular, Goebbels attempted to create toughness in the civilian population by resorting to one of the oldest techniques of persuasion—the indoctrination of fear. Fear of the subhuman Bolshevik "beast-man" endangering Western civilization ("strength through fear") together with "total war" became the leitmotivs of his propaganda during 1943.

Hitler's decline as the Party's leading speaker left a gap which Goebbels began to fill. By 1943, Goebbels had become the principal spokesman for the regime. It is interesting to note that in his speeches he adopted a posture similar to Winston Churchill; he made no secret of the difficulties ahead, admitted that a German defeat was possible, and called for total involvement in the war effort. It is somewhat ironic to see the master of the "lie indirect" suddenly discovering and openly proclaiming the tactical advantages of "absolute truth!" Proud of what he believed were his close contacts with the people, he adopted a pose of frankness and realism. However, after the catastrophe of Stalingrad, he was convinced of the need for some mass demonstration of national resistance. Strangely enough, the Allied demand for "unconditional surrender" conceived at the Casablanca Conference in January 1943 would provide just the impetus he needed. He could now use this to conjure up terrifying images of a nation fighting for its very existence. Total war, he could argue, was the only alternative to total destruction. Writing in his diary on March 4, 1943, Goebbels declared, "Our slogan should be, now more than ever: Total War Is the Imperative Need of the Hour."

Thus, in the aftermath of military disaster, the propaganda minister achieved a remarkable personal victory. The huge rally to an audience of 14,000 at the Sportspalast in Berlin on February 18, 1943, was the setting for his notorious "total war" address. It was a masterpiece in mass propaganda, carefully orchestrated for the benefit of radio, press, and the newsreel. Testimonies recorded by Goebbels himself and those around him also provide both witting and unwitting evidence of the cynical nature of the propaganda exercise. Rudolf Semmler, one of Goebbels's aids at the RMVP, recorded the propaganda minister's preparations for the event:

> Goebbels is brooding over a daring plan. He will try to bring pressure on Hitler by putting forward radical demands in a speech at the Sports Palace. The crowd

will applaud wildly. In this way he may be able to force Hitler to put an end to half measures. If his demands are not met then the government will be compromised. The Führer could not afford this at the moment.[1]

The audience of reliable party functionaries had been meticulously rehearsed beforehand and knew exactly what was expected of them. Goebbels started his speech by saying that the situation reminded him of the *Kampfzeit*, the period of struggle before 1933. He said he now demanded even more effort and sacrifices from the German people for the sake of final victory. Above the speaker's platform there hung an immense draped banner with the words *Totaler Krieg—Kürzester Krieg* ("Total War—Shortest War"). It was claimed that the audience represented all sections of the community. The frenzied reactions of this "representative" audience to Goebbels's speech were broadcast to the rest of the nation. A special newsreel also recorded the event. At the climax of the speech, the propaganda minister posed 10 questions touted as a "plebiscite for Total War," all of which elicited the appropriate chorus of "spontaneous" assent. The following extract is how it was presented to German cinema audiences in the *Deutsche Wochenschau* (German newsreel), which was released on February 27, 1943:

Commentator: The mighty demonstration in the Berlin Sportspalast, Reichminister Goebbels speaks. He declares: "In this winter, the storm over our ancient continent has broken out with the full force which surpasses all human and historical imagination. The Wehrmacht with its allies form the only possible protective wall. (Applause.) Not a single person in Germany today thinks of hollow compromise. The whole nation thinks only of a hard war. The danger before which we stand is gigantic. Gigantic, therefore, must be the efforts with which we meet it. (Shouts of 'Sieg Heil'.) When my audience spontaneously declared its support for the demands I made on 30 January, the English press claimed that this was a piece of theatrical propaganda. I have therefore invited to this meeting a cross-section of the German people . . ."

Goebbels: The English claim that the German people are resisting Government measures for total war.

Crowd: Lies! Lies!

Goebbels: It doesn't want total war, say the English, but capitulation.

Crowd: Sieg Heil! Sieg Heil!

Goebbels: Do you want total war?

Crowd: Yes. (Enthusiastic applause.)

Goebbels: Do you want it more total, more radical, than we could ever have imagined?

Crowd: Yes! Yes! (Loud applause.)

Goebbels:	Are you ready to stand with the Führer as the phalanx of the home-land behind the fighting Wehrmacht? Are you ready to continue the struggle unshaken and with savage determination, through all the vicissitudes of fate until victory is in our hands?
Crowd:	Yes!
Goebbels:	I ask you: Are you determined to follow the Führer through thick and thin in the struggle for victory and to accept even the harshest personal sacrifices?
Crowd:	Yes! Sieg Heil! (A chant of "The Führer commands, we follow.")
Goebbels:	You have shown our enemies what they need to know, so that they will no longer indulge in illusions. The mightiest ally in the world—the people themselves—have shown that they stand behind us in our determined fight for victory, regardless of the costs.
Crowd:	Yes! Yes! (Loud applause.)
Goebbels:	Therefore let the slogan be from now on: "People arise, and storm, break loose!" (Extended applause.)
Crowd:	Deutschland, Deutschland uber alles, uber alles in der Welt . . .

In his aforementioned "total war" speech, Goebbels pulled out all the stops; total sacrifices and participation are put forward by Goebbels as the alternatives to the type of total destruction that only the Wehrmacht were preventing. Partly, this was to convince foreign governments that there was full accord between the rulers and the ruled in Germany, but it was also intended to persuade Hitler to completely mobilize the home front to facilitate a concentrated war effort. On February 19 (the day after the event), Goebbels wrote in his diary:

> Many people are of the opinion that this mass meeting is really a type of *coup d'état.* But we are simply straddling the many hurdles which the bureaucracy has placed in our path. Total war is no longer just a question on the minds of a few perceptive men, but the whole nation is concerned with it.[2]

Albert Speer, who attended the rally and was Hitler's armaments minister, recorded its impact and the cynicism that shaped Goebbels's methods:

> On February 18, 1943, Goebbels delivered his speech at the Sportspalast on "Total War." It was not only directed to the population; it was obliquely addressed to the leadership which had ignored all our proposals for a radical commitment of domestic reserves. . . . Except for Hitler's most powerful public meetings, I had never seen an audience so effectively roused to fanaticism. Back in his home, Goebbels astonished me by analysing what had seemed to be a purely emotional outburst in terms of its psychological effects—much as an experienced actor might have done. He was also satisfied with his audience that evening. "Did

you notice? They reacted to the smallest nuance and applauded at just the right moments. It was the politically best-trained audience you can find in Germany." This particular crowd had been rounded up out of the party organisations; among those present were popular intellectuals and actors like Heinrich George whose applause was caught by the newsreel cameras for the benefit of the wider public.[3]

Although Hitler personally congratulated Goebbels on his address and referred to it as a "psychological and propaganda masterpiece," he would, however, never agree to complete mobilization, despite repeated requests from his propaganda minister. Nevertheless, in the short term at least, Goebbels enjoyed considerable success with this campaign. Its immediate effect served to strengthen morale. The Secret Police (SD) reports noted that the newsreel of the rally "made a deep impression and subsequently dissipated any feelings of skepticism which have prevailed up until now. Even rather reticent sections of the population were aroused when they saw the ecstatic effect of the speech." But once this intoxication had worn off, people began to question soberly the nature and implications of the threat coming from the East. The "total war" campaign served to lift morale at a time of widespread war-weariness and gave the false impression of a people at one with its leadership. In fact, the "success" of this campaign was short lived and raised expectations not of final victory but of a swift end to the war by means of a negotiated peace.

Notes

1. R. Semmler, *Goebbels: The Man Next to Hitler* (London: Westhouse, 1947), entry for January 29, 1943, 68.

2. E. Fröhlich (ed.), *Die Tagebucher von Joseph Goebbels*, vol. 2 (Munich: Ort Verlag, 1993), 370–375.

3. A. Speer, *Inside the Third Reich* (London: Sphere, 1971), 354.

Chapter 11

Women at War

The experience of World War I had shown the imperative need to mobilize civilians for industrial and labor purposes. In Britain, the government reacted immediately by granting itself power to direct civilians to perform service essential to the war effort. Early in 1941, legislation was passed requiring all men over 41 and women over 20 to register for employment in war work. One of the most controversial measures was the decision to conscript women for war work because of the shortage of labor. In December 1941, legislation was passed providing for conscription of women into the women's armed forces and in areas like civil defense and industry. They could, however, choose which service to enter. The new law applied to those between 20 and 30 but excluded married women. In 1942, official propaganda urged women to become "part of the DRIVING FORCE behind the Offensive" by joining the ATS (Auxiliary territorial Service) and the WAAF (Women's Auxiliary Air Force).

ABRAM GAMES'S STRIKING RECRUITMENT POSTER FOR THE MINISTRY OF INFORMATION (1943)

Document

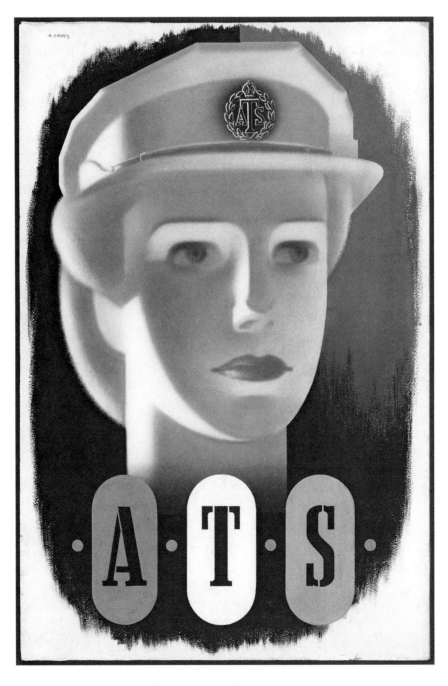

Source: U.K. National Archives, INF3/113.

Analysis

Some of Britain's most iconic images were produced by Abram Games. From 1942, Games was employed as an official war artist and produced over 100 posters, many dealing with the recruitment of women into the work-force and the armed forces. Games's style consisted of striking color, bold graphic ideas, and imaginatively integrated typography. One of his first posters was a recruitment poster for the ATS ("Join the ATS") nicknamed the "Blonde Bomb-shell," which led to attacks in parliament and its subsequent withdrawal on the grounds that it was too glamorous. The poster in Document 17 from 1944 is more restrained but equally effective. Note that the design is absolutely central to the propaganda message rendering any wording or slogan superfluous. By the end of 1942, more than 8.5 million women had registered for national service. By mid-1943, women constituted 40 percent of all employees in the aircraft industry, 35 percent in the engineering industry, and 52 percent in factories making explosives and chemicals.

The British mobilization for total war turned out to be far more successful than that of Germany and was largely built on the principle of consent, unlike the Nazi war effort, which relied on the exploitation of forced labor from the occupied countries. In Nazi Germany, the Labor Law of 1935 and 1939 requiring young women as well as young men to work in industrial and agricultural jobs was not systematically enforced because of Hitler's opposition to German women working, and because Germany utilized forced labor from the occupied territories. As we have seen from Joseph Goebbels's Total War speech in February 1943 (see Document 16), although he secured briefly a propaganda coup of sort, Hitler would never agree to complete mobilization of women for the workforce or the armed forces. Although during the final year of the war, more than 500,000 German women served as volunteer uniformed auxiliaries in the German armed forces.

In the Soviet Union, posters were rarely used to enlist women. Although Soviet women were heavily involved in war work, posters were used to raise morale by conveying in patriotic slogans their contribution to the war effort. Typical are Alexei Kokorekin's "Weapons for the Front from the Soviet Women" (1942), showing a stern female munitions worker standing guard over an assembly line of recently manufactured bombs; and in a different fashion, "A tractor in the field is worth a tank in battle" (Viktor Ivanov and Olga Burova, 1942) depicting a calm, orderly nation where Russian women are shown ploughing the fields for food, while tanks and other military weapon are sent to the front via the Soviet rail network. In contrast to Britain, America, and many other allies, the Soviet Union and Nazi Germany were aesthetically and ideologically opposed to allow women's war work to be perceived as "glamorous."

American women entered the workforce in unprecedented numbers during World War II, as widespread male enlistment left gaping holes in the industrial labor force. The U.S. posters recruiting women for war work attempted to show them in various industrial plants where 2 million women were employed by 1942 and 5 million by 1945. Between 1940 and 1945, the female percentage of the U.S. workforce increased from 27 percent to nearly 37 percent, and by 1945, nearly one out of every four married women worked outside the home. The most famous and iconic figure was "Rosie the Riveter" (in Britain, there was "Eve in Overalls"). Based in small part on a real-life munitions worker, but primarily a fictitious character, the strong, bandanna-clad Rosie became one of the most successful recruitment tools in American history, and the most iconic image of working women in the World War II era.[1] In 1942, J. Howard Miller was hired by the Westinghouse Company's War Production Coordinating Committee to create a series of posters for the war effort. One of these posters became the famous "We Can Do It!" image of a determined female armaments worker flexing her muscles. The purpose of Miller's poster was to maintain production quotas by boosting morale, not to recruit more women workers.

In addition to munitions work and other home front jobs, some 350,000 women joined the armed services, serving at home and abroad. At the urging of First Lady Eleanor Roosevelt and women's groups, and impressed by the British use of women in service, General George Marshall supported the idea of introducing a women's service branch into the Army. In May 1942, Congress instituted the Women's Auxiliary Army Corps, later upgraded to the Women's Army Corps, which had full military status. Its members, known as WACs, worked in more than 200 noncombatant jobs stateside and in every theater of the war. By 1945, there were more than 100,000 WACs and 6,000 female officers. In the Navy, members of Women Accepted for Volunteer Emergency Service (WAVES) held the same status as naval reservists and provided support stateside. The Coast Guard and Marine Corps soon followed suit, though in smaller numbers.

Document 18

"RONNIE, THE BREN GUN GIRL" (CANADA, 1941)

Document

Source: National Film Board of Canada. Photothèque/Library and Archives Canada/PA-119766.

Analysis

The use of similar images of women engaged in war work or enlisting in the armed forces appeared in other countries such as Britain and Canada (a British variant on "Rosie" was "Eve in Overalls"). Document 18 is an official publicity photograph of "Ronnie, the Bren Gun Girl," the Canadian precursor to "Rosie the Riveter." Posing with a finished Bren gun at the John Inglis Company plant in Toronto where she worked, this photo is an excellent example of official government coverage of workers at home during World War II. First produced in 1937, the Bren gun became one of the most widely used machine guns of its kind and was a staple for line troops during World War II. Veronica Foster, popularly known as "Ronnie, the Bren Gun Girl," was a Canadian icon representing nearly 1 million Canadian women who worked in the munition plants that produced munitions and material during World War II. Veronica Foster is depicted here as in other photos posing in a provocative (or emancipatory) manner, caressing the Bren gun while exhaling cigarette smoke. "Ronnie" became popular after a series of propaganda posters were produced; most images featured her working for the war effort ("Ronnie Says, 'Keep 'em Coming!' for Victory") but others depicted more informal intimate settings *after* work, like Foster dancing the jitterbug or attending official functions. Serving as both an inspiration for Canadian women, while simultaneously as a sex symbol for the troops in the field, her image and her choice as a symbol in the war effort had been carefully cultivated and perfectly accomplished.

Generally speaking, women played a vital part in World War II, although their roles varied from country to country. But, as with the aftermath in World War I, women at the end of 1945, found that the advances they had made were greatly reduced when the soldiers returned from fighting abroad. Postwar, women were returned to many of the mundane jobs they occupied before the war started. Where once the manufacturing factories and the armed forces represented an escape from domestic life and liberty, they now returned to the male-dominated field they were before the war.[2]

Notes

1. "Rosie" as popularized in a song of the same name that in 1942 became a hit for bandleader Kay Kyser. Soon afterward, Walter Pidgeon, a Hollywood leading man, traveled to the Willow Run aircraft plant in Ypsilanti, Michigan, to make a promotional film encouraging the sale of war bonds. One of the women employed at the factory, Rose Will Monroe, was a riveter involved in the construction of B-24 and B-29 bombers. Monroe, a real-life Rosie the Riveter, was recruited to appear in Pidgeon's film.

2. For general histories of the role played by women in World War II see, D. Weatherford, *American Women during World War II* (New York: Routledge, 2010); L. J. Rupp, *Mobilizing Women for War: German and American Propaganda, 1939–1945* (Princeton, NJ: Princeton University Press, 1979); K. Hagemann, "Mobilizing Women for War: The History, Historiography, and Memory of German Women's War Service in the Two World Wars," *Journal of Military History* (2011), 75–74, 1055–1094; K. Jean Cottam, "Soviet Women in Combat in World War II: The Ground Forces and the Navy," *International Journal of Women's Studies*, vol. 3, no. 4 (1980), 345–357; B. Williams, *Women at War (World at War—World War II)* (Oxford: Heinemann, 2006).

Chapter 12

Keeping Healthy and Personal Hygiene

Coughs and Sneezes Spread Diseases

Total War meant that civilians in the home front had to be physically fit in order to fight, work efficiently and to cope with air raids, and generally endure the discomforts caused by shortages of food and fuel. In 1943, Britain's Minister of Health, Ernest Brown, was responsible for the booklet *How to Keep Well in Wartime*, which offered commonsense advice on a range of health issues such as proper exercise, excessive smoking and drinking, and the importance of a good diet. A major concern for the British authorities was the spread of germs, resulting in large-scale absenteeism from work. In his pamphlet, Bevin had noted: ". . . as a nation we are still losing about 22 million weeks' work each year through common and often preventable illness." Among other advice, the booklet urged people to cough or sneeze into a handkerchief and denounced any failure to do so as a "rude and disgusting habit." One of the most famous wartime poster slogans read: "Coughs and Sneezes Spread Diseases." Popular film stars and celebrities were recruited to add weight to these health campaigns.

Document 19

"COUGHS AND SNEEZES SPREAD DISEASES"
(GB, CIRCA 1942)

Document

Source: National Archives/SSPL/Getty Images.

Analysis

The propaganda campaign, which was coordinated by the Ministry of Information and spearheaded by a series of eight posters, was designed to show how thoughtlessness helped to spread not only the common cold but also many other diseases. Document 19 is one of the series of eight issued by the Ministry of Health (circa 1942), showing the effects of coughs and sneezes in various everyday situations. In this poster, the figures are actually drawn on a handkerchief—to reinforce the message. The workers queuing in a works canteen (note the desert menu: "jam roll, rice pudding, prunes and custard") are visibly shocked and annoyed when a selfish individual sneezes over a work colleague who is forced to drop his spoon. There is a certain humor in the style of the drawing, very much in the tradition of risqué British seaside postcards. But the message was deadly serious. In 1943, a Ministry of Information newsreel intended to encourage more hygienic habits in the population as a whole, showed scenes of every aspect of wartime Britain; in workplaces, factories, homes, public places such as concerts and cinemas selfish individuals are shown coughing and sneezing without resorting to a handkerchief to catch their germs. The final scene of the newsreel is intended to bring home to the home front just how damaging absenteeism is to the war effort; a printed warning appears on the screen in capital letters: "Time lost through colds and 'flu each year is equivalent in production to—3,500 TANKS and 1000 BOMBERS and 1,000,0000 RIFLES . . . Trap the germs in your handkerchief . . . HELP TO KEEP THE NATION FIGHTING FIT!" Like many of the posters, the message is largely disseminated with a light touch. It was considered important not to overtly lecturing the people who were making the sacrifices but to encourage.

Indeed, the whole "coughs and sneezes" campaign, which extended beyond World War II, was far more to do with fighting absenteeism than concern about people catching an ordinary cold. According to the Mass Observation research project, the poster campaign proved particularly effective with simple messages such as "Remember a handkerchief in time saves nine—and helps to keep the nation fighting fit," "Wanted for Sneezing to the Public Danger—and coughing without due care and attention," and "The Ministry of Health says: Coughs and Sneezes Spread Diseases. Trap the germs in your handkerchief."[1]

Personal Hygiene

During both the world wars, one particular health problem singled out was the need to combat venereal disease (VD) by avoiding casual sexual intercourse. *Keep Well in Wartime* warned: "A hospital full of cases of gonorrhea means loss of tanks, loss of aeroplanes, loss of guns. It also means loss of happiness, loss of health, loss of efficiency." It was assumed that men fighting far away from their home and families would be prone to sexual temptation. During World War I, for example, sexually transmitted diseases caused the U.S. Army to lose the services of 18,000 servicemen per day. During World War II, preventative efforts intensified through films, lectures, posters, leaflets, and the greater availability of condoms. The U.S. propaganda posters targeted at soldiers and sailors appealed to their patriotism in urging them to protect themselves, with such slogans as "You can't be at the Axis if you get VD." Images of women were used to catch the eye on many VD posters, combined with a message that had to be unequivocal: "She may look clean—But . . . Pick Ups, 'Good Time' Girls, Prostitutes—Spread Syphilis and Gonorrhoea." (Such efforts were not confined to the United States, of course. For example, in the Soviet Union the great filmmaker Alexander Medvedkin was producing films for the Red Army, including the hygiene film *Watch Your Health*, 1927.)

Infection rates remained stubbornly high, but treatment times were drastically reduced with the arrival of penicillin. Cases of venereal disease even gained priority access to drugs if that meant a faster return to the frontline. By 1944, the number of men lost to service had been reduced 30-fold (though there were still around 600 servicemen incapacitated every day). This drop in numbers was partly because of the U.S. Army's effort to raise awareness about the dangers faced by servicemen through poor sexual hygiene, and the war department supplied each recruit, on enlistment, with a 16-page leaflet titled "Sex Hygiene and Venereal Diseases." The other important factor lay in the medical advances. In late 1943, a case of gonorrhea required a hospital treatment of 30 days, and curing syphilis remained a 6-month ordeal; by mid-1944, the average case of gonorrhea was reduced to a treatment of 5 days, and in many cases the patient remained on duty status, while being treated.[2]

All combatant nations in the war designed their own campaigns to warn military and civilian personnel of the dangers of sexually transmitted diseases. Such diseases were depicted as yet another enemy that soldiers were called on to fight against. One such American poster shows a woman in the center of a group of men, who are all staring at her amorously. The text below the woman says: "V-Gals. The victory girls are on the loose and soon will cook some poor guy's goose. The G.I. Joes must be more wary of the diseases they may carry. Venereal disease is on the rise. So take your pros; be well and wise!"

At the same time that there were printing posters, the U.S. government also produced a number of pamphlets, flyers, leaflets, and other published literature in an attempt to slow the rate of VD among the troops. The war department issued a 16-page brochure titled "Sex Hygiene and VD—Venereal Disease." It was first printed in 1940 under the direction of the surgeon general of the Army with an introduction by Secretary of War George Marshall. It was issued to every new recruit and discusses sexuality in general and attempts to educate the young soldier on all of the emotions and desires he might encounter away from home. Another booklet, War Department Pamphlet No. 21–15, depicts American troops hitting the beaches from a landing craft on some foreign shore and warns that VD might take them out of the picture.

"HELLO BOY FRIEND, COMING MY WAY?"
(GB, VENEREAL DISEASE POSTER, CIRCA 1943)

Document

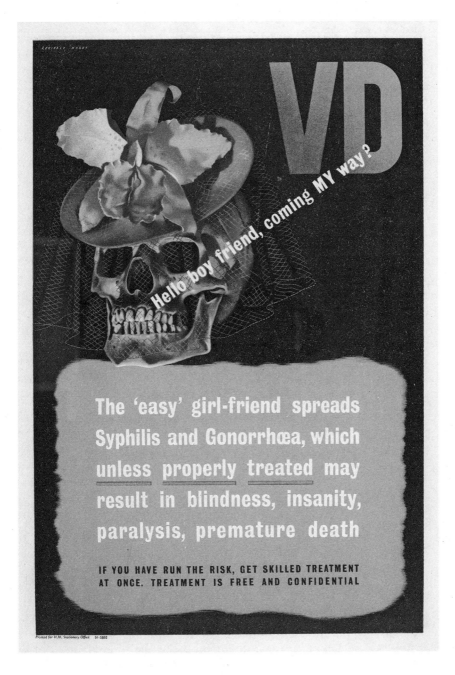

Source: Imperial War Museum (IWM_PST_000800_A), © IWM.

Analysis

Document 20, a provocatively colorful VD poster produced in Britain by the artist Reginald Mount for the Ministry of Information (MOI) depicted a skull wearing a bright pink bonnet, its ironically tempting text inviting the reader: "Hello boy friend, coming MY way?" A lurid evocation of the disabling and potentially fatal threats lurking beneath the superficial glamour of the "'easy' girl-friend" as a VD source is conveyed in this British poster.[3] The skull gives an indication of the "kiss of death," smiling as it beckons the man toward the faceless "easy" woman. The veil adds a furtive atmosphere to all this, suggesting that the true nature of the woman cannot be seen, that she is behaving in a "shady" manner, as a prostitute would. Forming part of a wider 1943–1944 anti-VD campaign—when it was discovered that the total incidence of venereal diseases were 139 percent higher than in 1939—both the imagery and the message in this poster are intended to shock the target audience and to act as a deterrent. The repercussions of contacting VD are spelt out in stark detail ("blindness, insanity, paralysis, premature death"). However, the equally important message is that treatment is available (indeed "unless it is properly treated" is underlined in the poster's main message) for all those "who have run the risk"—and that it is free and confidential. Stylistically, the poster is of interest for its surrealistic features and can be compared to similar use made of surrealism and photomontage by other poster designers of World War II, notably Abram Games (See Document 17).

Such messages were far removed from the propaganda posters that encouraged women to participate in the war effort. A famous poster produced by the Americans in 1942 showed a women working in an armament factory with the title "Women in the War. We Can't Win Without Them."

In December 1942, Mass Observation questioned British people on press advertisements about sexually transmitted diseases. Half of them still seemed ignorant about the subject, and about 10 percent were embarrassed by it, with some men worried about their womenfolk viewing the subject in the newspapers. Few understood what the different venereal diseases were, although "the pox" and "the clap" were mentioned in responses—and in one case the "venerable" disease. The British government was roused into action and Document 20 was therefore part of the first national propaganda campaign on this subject, utilizing the press, radio, films, exhibitions, and posters.

Notes

1. The core slogan endured, and the campaign continues to be used by the National Health Service to this day, for example, being extensively exploited to prevent the spread of "swine flu" in 2009.

2. A.M. Brandt, *No Magic Bullet: A Social History of Venereal Disease in the United States since 1880* (Oxford University Press, Oxford, 1987).

3. As well as designing the poster, Mount also wrote the copy. Mount later wrote, "Research showed . . . this disease was not contracted only from prostitutes, but in

many cases from the 'easy' girl friend . . . I wanted to show that contact with this sort of female could be, quite literally, the kiss of death." He used the female skull (which he borrowed from a medical school) as the symbol of death, the flamboyant hat (hired) as the symbol of enticement, the orchid (an imitation one which he bought) for "a certain fleshly unhealthiness," and the veil for a feeling of furtiveness; the ensemble was painted as a still life over a series of days with a note left on the hat each night asking the cleaner not to disturb it. Quoted in J. Darracott and B. Loftus, *Second World War Posters*, 45.

Chapter 13

Buy War Bonds

The need to raise money to pay for the war by means of war bonds provided one of the most important propaganda themes for posters and the cinema. War loans and war saving stamps (which varied in price from a dime to $50) also helped governments to regulate war economies and limit inflation. They placed less emphasis on the value of buying bonds as a shrew financial investment than on the opportunity for civilians to contribute to the war effort directly. The first Series E U.S. Savings Bond was purchased by President Franklin D. Roosevelt on May 1, 1941.

A study of commercial posters undertaken by the U.S. government found that images of women and children in danger were effective emotional devices. Even after Pearl Harbor, the Office of War Information (OWI), deemed it necessary with so many American troops stationed in Europe, to stress that the totalitarian dictators in Southeast Asia and Europe, represented a real threat to the United States (interestingly, Mussolini and fascist Italy rarely figured in American propaganda as a major military threat). Public relations specialists advised the U.S. government that the most effective war posters were the ones that appealed to the emotions. Posters often played on the public's fear of the enemy. The images depict Americans in imminent danger—their backs against the wall, living in the shadow of Axis domination. One of the earliest posters in this genre was produced by the General Motors Corporation in 1942, which showed Hitler brandisher a luger pistol and a snarling Japanese soldier (presumably Emperor Hirohito) with blood dripping from a dagger leering at a map of the United States on the globe with the caption: "Warning! Our Homes Are in Danger *Now*!," with an insert of American bombers and a side caption that reads: "Our Job . . . Keep 'em Firing."

WAR BONDS POSTER: "KEEP THESE HANDS OFF!" "BUY THE NEW VICTORY BONDS" (CANADA, 1942, G. K. ODELL)

Document

Source: National Archives. Poster by G. K. Odell.

Analysis

Canada declared war on Nazi Germany on September 10, 1939, seven days after Britain and France.[1] Document 21 is a Canadian poster designed by G. K. Odell in 1942 and was part of the study that had been undertaken by the American government. In this poster, there are symbols on two claw-like hands, which represent Nazi Germany and the Empire of Japan. Both hands are reaching toward mother and baby. The vulnerability of the mother and child is emphasized by the exclamatory injunction to "Keep these hands off!" They are painted with pale, delicate colors while dark, witch-like hands threaten their security. The juxtaposition of colors and images were intended to illicit an emotional response by making the audience feel responsible for the well-being of women and children. In spite of the fact that women were making a major contribution to the war effort—both in and out of the armed services—this poster ignores contemporary reality and instead focuses on traditional images of female femininity and fragility. Odell's crude psychological employment of triggering highly emotional responses to images such as vulnerable women and children, served as a model for American posters such as the one below (Document 22) that adopted a similar visual theme.

WAR BONDS POSTER: "DON'T LET THAT SHADOW TOUCH THEM. BUY WAR BONDS" (USA, 1942, LAWRENCE B. SMITH)

Document

Source: National Archives. Poster by Lawrence B. Smith.

Analysis

The emphasis in this 1942 poster by Lawrence B. Smith for the OWI is on the all-American family; three children innocently playing—but with war toys and an American flag—and the shadow of the swastika menacingly stretching across their lawn ("Don't let that shadow touch them"). Similar to Odell's poster, the three children form the central image on the poster and all three look touchingly innocent and vulnerable to some looming threat. One boy holds a toy U.S. military airplane. Another boy wears a paper hat and holds an American flag on a makeshift pole. The girl is seated and holds a doll. She is sitting on a rock in front of the two boys with a look of confusion on her face. One hand is lifted in the air in uncertainty, and the other hand is holding the arm of a doll in a blue blouse. Her doll is lying like a corpse with its face turned toward the ground, and the little girl's eyes are fixated on the shadow of the swastika slowly inching over the doll's body. The smaller boy is dressed in blue shorts and a red and white striped shirt. He is wearing a hat made out of a newspaper and is holding up a flag the pole of which he seems to have put together himself. The expression on his face is frightened, as he looks to the older boy for guidance and safety. He is standing with a hand in front of the younger boy in a defensive and protective manner and is holding a toy U.S. airplane in the other hand. His eyes, focused on something in the sky, are clearly worried. The perspective of this picture is also of interest. The angle at which the audience is observing this scene is elevated, from the sky or even just the upstairs window of a house. The point is that the viewer is separated from these children by a distance. The shadow, however, is already there, and moving in on them. There is a real sense of urgency about this composition that suggest unless war bonds are not bought in sufficient numbers by American citizens it *might* be too late. Note that it is a middle class, white family. Although African Americans were fighting in the armed forces and contributing to the war effort at home, the majority of official propaganda at this time still concentrated on "white" America. This was not lost on black American leader both during and after the war.

The OWI produced a booklet titled *The Poster Handbook*, which made suggestions on how to display posters effectively ("posting of official governmental posters is one of the most valuable contributions which citizens can make to the war effort"). During the course of the war, the OWI commissioned a wide variety of war-bond posters that increasingly adopted more assertive and inspirational approaches. A vivid color poster from 1942 with the simple caption: "Buy War Bonds" inspires American civilians to actively participate. The poster features a representation of Uncle Sam amid U.S. air and land forces, carrying a billowing American flag over his shoulder. During World War II, bond sales were consistently successful and incrementally more ambitious. In May 1942, sales exceeded that month's goal of $800 million and for July $1 billion. Targets were invariably achieved and by the time the Fifth War Loan was launched on June 6, 1944 (D-Day), the target figure had been raised to $16 billion in bonds.[2] A feature of the 1943 campaign was an inserted shield in the posters, saying, "We bought extra war bonds/4th War Loan." Typical was the poster designed by Bernard Perlin of a GI lobbying a bomb at the enemy with the slogan: "Let 'em Have It . . . Buy *Extra* Bonds." For the Seventh War Loan in 1945, Dean Cornwell designed the American eagle perched on a pile of $200 bonds with the slogan: "Victory—now you can invest in it! Victory Loan." By the end of the war, 85 million Americans had invested in war bonds.[3]

Document 23
A JAPANESE "SAVE FOR VICTORY" CARTOON (1942–1944)

Document

Source: © The British Library Board.

Analysis

All the belligerents made similar appeals to their own citizens and employed every medium available. Document 23 is a Japanese "Save for Victory" cartoon (1942–1944). Stylistically, it is very different from the slick advertising methods employed by most of the other major belligerents in the war. Much softer in tone, President Roosevelt is depicted as a boxer wearing "Stars and Stripes" trunks and US-dollar boxing gloves. To the president's right, he is being dealt a knock-out blow by a traditional samurai Japanese warrior. This cartoon, like the Canadian and American posters carried the same propaganda message, that ordinary citizens could contribute to ultimate victory by saving for war bonds in order to finance their war effort. The message, based on national pride and fear of the enemy, inevitably prompted a positive response from citizens in all the fighting nations.

While the initial goal of selling war bonds was to finance the war, it had the positive side effect of raising morale on the home front. War loan posters were almost certainly the largest category of posters produced between 1939 and 1945 (the same applied in World War I). Following the approaches of other propaganda campaigns, war loan posters appealed to patriotism and historical identity and occasionally played on the sense of guilt that might be experienced by those who did not fight.

Notes

1. By the war's end, over 1 million citizens would serve in military uniform (out of a prewar population of 11 million), and Canada would possess the fourth-largest air force and third-largest naval surface fleet in the world. Around 41 percent of Canadian males 18–45 served in the military during 1939–1945. P. C. Stacey, *Arms, Men and Governments: The War Policies of Canada, 1939–1945* (Ottawa: Queen's Printer, 1970).

2. Figures cited in D. Nelson, *The Posters That Won the War* (Osceola, WI: Motorbooks, 1991), 146–147.

3. All seven war loans met their target, although most of the money that the U.S. government received came from banks, corporations, and insurance companies.

Chapter 14

Posting Propaganda

The Postage Stamp

An often neglected medium of propaganda iconography is the postage stamp. The stamp proved an ideal vehicle for propaganda in World War II and was used by all the belligerents. Postage stamps are part of the "everyday," and few people associate the humble stamp with government propaganda.

The outbreak of war in 1939 brought immediate propaganda changes within the Soviet Union. Following the signing of the Nonaggression Pact with Germany, while the Soviet Union began to present itself as a "champion of peace" in order to explain away its surprising *volte face* with its sworn ideological enemy, it also started to prepare the nation for war. The armed forces were greatly expanded. An indication of this change was the issue of postage stamps depicting Soviet military power. Stamps now showed the Red Army taking up arms as well as Soviet aircraft engaged in military action and adoring Soviet citizens waving Soviet tanks into action (Document 24).

SOVIET POSTAGE STAMPS (1940): "WELCOME TO THE RED ARMY" AND A CROWD WAVING AT SOVIET TANKS

Document

Source: artnana/Shutterstock.com.

Analysis

Following the initially successful Operation Barbarossa in June 1941, the Soviets now found themselves allied with the Western democracies. Postage stamps now depicted the Big Three leaders in fraternal discussion with the national flags of their countries intertwined above their heads. At the same time, the Soviet government reduced its emphasis on the international nature of communism so as not to offend their new allies. In order to strengthen the people's will to resist, postage stamps, together with films and posters, appealed to their patriotism rather than their communism (Documents 24 and 25). It was no coincidence that Stalin coined the new struggle "the great patriotic war."[1]

Document 25

A SOVIET POSTAGE STAMP (1941) FOLLOWING THE NAZI INVASION: "BE A HERO!"

Document

Source: Post of the Soviet Union, Russian Federation.

Analysis

The stamp proved an ideal vehicle for Nazi propaganda, and it was used to mark events in the Nazi calendar from the War Hero's Day (1935) to the production of the "people's car" (*Volkswagen*), and the 1936 Olympic Games. Stamps were also used to commemorate Hitler himself. Interestingly enough, however, Hitler's portrait did not appear on an official Reichpost stamp until 1937. Thereafter, special stamps were issued nearly every year to celebrate Hitler's birthday. The 1939 issue was a striking black-and-white design of Hitler in dramatic pose as the all-powerful orator, speaking from the podium. In 1940, with Germany at war, a gentler image of Hitler was issued of the Führer affectionately greeting a small child carrying a bouquet of flowers (Document 26). After 1940, further issues depicted Hitler in military uniform in the pose of *Feldherr*. This series was also issued in the occupied territories.

Document 26

A GERMAN STAMP COMMEMORATING HITLER'S BIRTHDAY (1940)

Document

Source: Alex Churilov/Shutterstock.com

Analysis

Propaganda also played an important role in the projection of the leader figure in Fascist Italy. Italian propaganda depicted Benito Mussolini as "Il Duce," a protean superman whose powers were unlimited. Mussolini was well aware of the importance of this role and played up to such an image. Official posters, films and postages stamps were used to project Mussolini (normally in formal fascist paramilitary uniform) and to commemorate fascist organizations and achievements in a similar fashion to that of Nazi Germany. Fascism demanded authority from above, obedience from below and this is expressed in the slogan: "Believe, Obey, Fight." When the Ministry of Popular Culture (*Miniculpop*) was established in June 1937, the Italian Fascists were finally able to coordinate all means of communication and disseminate propaganda tightly controlled by the party. Following Mussolini's illegal invasion of Abyssinia (Ethiopia) in October 1936, he increasingly aligned himself with Hitler, which resulted in the Rome-Berlin Axis of 1936 and the military "Pact of Steel" of May 1939. In June 1940, Mussolini declared war in support of Germany and invaded France. Document 27 shows two postage stamps issued by the Italian government in 1940 in commemoration of the Rome-Berlin Axis. The first stamp consists of profiles of Hitler and Mussolini with their respective fascist symbols (the Nazi eagle perched on a swastika and the Italian dagger and *fasci* [axe]) with the words: "Two Peoples, One War."

ITALIAN POSTAGE STAMPS (1940) HITLER AND MUSSOLINI: "TWO PEOPLES, ONE WAR"

Document

Source: withGod/Shutterstock.com.

Analysis

These stamps were issued to celebrate the early joint military successes experienced by the Fascist states in Europe. However, as the war turned against Italy, the economic conditions at home only exacerbated the growing resentment at what was perceived as the over-reliance on Germany.

Later in the war, the black propaganda section of the British Political Warfare Executive (PWE) under Sefton Delmer (See "Black" Propaganda), played on Italian resentment by issuing a British "black" parody stamp paraphrasing Mussolini's slogan: "Two nations, One War," as "two nations, one Führer." The "black" parody, which was probably prepared in the fall of 1943, calls attention to the fact that Hitler is in full charge of the Axis partnership. In this version, Hitler is snarling at a surprised Mussolini whose ceremonial axe and dagger are also chipped. Within a few months of this issue, the Grand Council of Fascism voted Mussolini out of office.

The Postcard

World War II had given the picture postcard a new lease of life. Prior to 1914, the picture postcard was the television of its day. Postcards throughout World War II remained popular because they were cheap to produce and writing letters and postcards formed a major communications plank in the everyday life of the communities of all the belligerent states. Postcards of World War II covered every conceivable theme and emotions; they were satirical, they could be bitter, they idealized leaders and military heroes, they employed humor and patriotism. There main function, however, was to raise morale.

Document 28
ITALIAN POSTCARD (CIRCA 1942)

Document

Source: The Welch Collection.

Analysis

Governments were particularly keen that military personnel fighting abroad should be kept in constant contact with family and loved ones. To this end, most of the belligerent nations provided patriotic postcards free of charge for the military. Document 28 is an example of a government-sponsored postcard for the armed forces. No stamp was required, but soldiers, sailors, and airmen invariably had to provide their rank and military unit on the back of the postcard. Postcards remained, however, subject to strict military censorship. Document 28 is an Italian postcard that relies entirely on a simple, visual composition to stir patriotic emotions. The postcard tells its own patriotic story and required no slogans. In this case, an Italian tank above which flies the flags of the Axis powers—Italy, Nazi Germany, and Japan. Both the tank and the flags emerge from a blast of light that illuminates the sky. The tank can be seen crushing the flags of Britain, America, and the Soviet Union. The propaganda message was simple, and the visual narrative was unequivocal: the Axis powers were winning the war. Postcards proved an extraordinarily vivid contemporary and simple communication medium that encouraged the fighting and home fronts to write to each other and, in so doing, "post" their patriotic propaganda.

Document 29

JOSEPH GOEBBELS: THIRTY ARTICLES OF WAR FOR THE GERMAN PEOPLE (SEPTEMBER 26, 1943)

Document

These are the articles of war for the German people, who are now engaged in the most fateful battle of their history. Countless of Germany's best have sacrificed their lives in their spirit both at the front and at home for the life and freedom of their nation. Millions of brave German soldiers fight for them on every front, and millions of industrious men and woman work untiringly for them at home, in the factories, workshops, offices, laboratories, and in agriculture.

These war articles are a reminder to our people of those who have fallen. They are a testimony to the willingness of those who fight and work to sacrifice, and a harsh rebuke to the lazy and undecided.

Article 1

Everything is possible in this war, save that we capitulate and bow to the power of the enemy. Anyone who speaks or even thinks in such a way is a cowardly traitor, and must be expelled in disgrace and shame from the fighting and working German community.

Article 2

We are fighting for our lives. If we win, we will be able to repair the damage and the pain this war has caused in a relatively short time by applying our full strength. If we lose, it will mean the end of our nation and our history.

Article 3

This war is a defensive war. It was forced upon us by our enemies, who wish to destroy the possibility of life and growth for our nation. If they succeed, our present generation will have lost everything that countless German generations have won over millennia of struggle by hard work and sacrifice. Our nation's history will end in shame and disgrace.

Article 4

This war brings countless dangers and risks, as does any war. Each must remember that every danger and risk can be overcome if a great nation like Germany with a capable and determined leadership uses all its strength and every resource to deal with it.

Article 5

We will certainly win this war if all Germans think of the community and act as do the best sons of our people. But if all ignored the community, as do the lazy, the cowardly, and the hesitant, we would have long since lost it. The war will be won or lost according to the strength of our community.

Article 6

Each German proves his community sense by conscientiously fulfilling his duties to the nation, just as he makes a claim on the community. Even in times of peace, each is dependent on the help and support of the community, and must therefore also be willing to share its burdens and duties. How much more is that true during war!

Article 7

Any advice from the enemy is an attack on our war morale. The enemy wants to win as much as we do. Everything he says and does is intended to lead us astray and deceive us. He who listens to the enemy, no matter how sanctimonious the reasons he may give, puts his people in the gravest danger. Ignorance may not protect him from the penalty he deserves.

Article 8

Silence is an important command from the war leadership. Few know the war's secrets. These are weapons in our nation's struggle for existence, and may not be revealed to the enemy. It would be unfair and destructive of the general welfare to spread rumors that force the government to speak about matters important or even decisive in the war. This can only help the enemy and harm our nation.

Article 9

The war leadership is doing the best it can. Often it cannot reveal the reasons for its actions without giving valuable information to the enemy. That means that even those of good will often do not understand its actions. That is why it must have the confidence of the people, confidence it has earned by its courage, cleverness, farsightedness, as well as its past successes. The know-it-alls can criticize only because the government is condemned to silence; if it could speak, they would be refuted instantly.

Article 10

The only thing we cannot afford to lose in this war is our freedom, the foundation of our life and our future. Everything else can be replaced, even if only through years of hard work. But a loss of our freedom would mean the loss of all our other material and cultural possessions, both for the nation as a whole and for each individual. If the war requires it, we must therefore be willing to use all we have to defend that freedom. Without it, neither the nation nor the individual can live.

Article 11

An old trick of warfare is to split a people from its government, leaving it leaderless and therefore defenseless. This is the only trick with which the enemy could defeat us. Anyone who falls prey to the enemy's trick is either stupid or a traitor. He endangers the victory for which our soldiers risk their lives, and for which our heroes have died. He stabs the fighting front in the back. No penalty is too severe for him.

Article 12

Beware of those seemingly intelligent people who seek to win your confidence with clever words, then undermine your confidence with a flood of phrases and rumors. Listen carefully to what they say, and you will soon see that they are cowardly, not intelligent. They may know better, but they cannot do better. Were they the latter, instead of criticizing they would be filling an important position at home or at the front, contributing by their actions to speeding our victory.

Article 13

He who speaks about the war and its prospects should always speak as if the enemy were listening. In many cases, he actually is. Each thoughtless word from our side gives him new hope and courage, and therefore prolongs the war. Annoyance or anger about this or that inconvenience of the war sometimes has justification, but in view of the great battle we stand in the midst of, most problems are of minor significance,

Article 14

We are helping those who need it as much as possible. If real help is impossible during the war, those affected should know that it will come after victory. Victory is the prerequisite for a national reconstruction that will repair all the damage of the war. The more one sacrifices for the war, the more fanatically one believes in victory. Therefore we must work and fight. That alone gives sacrifices, even the hardest ones, their meaning.

Article 15

Each must, therefore, follow to the letter all the laws and regulations related to the war. Who violates them from neglect or forgetfulness does just as much damage as if he did so intentionally. Each must take the war with the serious-ness it deserves.

Article 16

Anything grows dull with time, even the impact of the war. We must therefore constantly guard against becoming lackadaisical in fulfilling our war duties. Our behavior today will be admired in a few decades by our children and grandchildren. They will not experience the spiritual pain that this long war has brought us. Rather, they will see the war only as the greatest heroic event in the history of our nation. Do not forget that in the midst of the everyday problems of the war.

Article 17

Everything comes to an end eventually, even war. We must be sure that its end is a happy one. We can best ensure that by remaining calm and steadfast. The nation with the most of these virtues will win.

Article 18

Nothing is more stupid than to believe that the leadership has it better than the people. The individual may have a heavy material burden to carry. But the heaviest burden is that of responsibility, with its never-ending cares. One should not be unfair and should not make unreasonable judgments about matters he does not understand.

Article 19

Nothing is more contemptible than to think that one part of the nation wages the war, and another only watches. This is no war of governments or armies, it is a war of peoples. He who stands aside only proves that he does not understand the situation. He is a war parasite who lives from the pain and contributions of others. Were they to think as he, we would lose the war. In the interests of decent citizens, the lazy must be reminded of their war duties. The war effort demands that, as does public morale.

Article 20

Just as in war there are medals and decorations for those who fulfill their duties with distinction, so, too, there must be warnings and if necessary harsh penalties for those who neglect their war duties. A war duty left undone is far worse than a neglected duty in time of peace. Each German today lives under the laws of war. They lay out harsh penalties, even for behaviors that are not all that serious in peace. They are shameful crimes during war, since they endanger victory. They deserve the harshest penalties.

Article 21

The soldier dies at the front while fulfilling his duty. He has the right to demand that those at home who sabotage or harm the war effort receive the death penalty. The front has the right to be supported by high morale at home. Anyone whose actions at home rob the front of this assurance deserves a harsh penalty. The soldier at the front demands it.

Article 22

Whether at home or at the front, discipline is the most important virtue. We can master the war's enormous problems only through iron resolve. A weakness in discipline weakens morale and violates all the laws of war. Any loosening of our people's unity in war is a crime against the community. Our people's greatest chance of victory is in firm resolve and hard determination.

Article 23

No one has the right to complain about limitations on his personal freedom caused by the war. What significance do these have in view of the fact that countless men, even woman and children, have died!

Article 24

The war demands our full devotion for itself and its duties. All that still remains from can only be viewed as a gift subject to recall. We must always realize that sooner or later we may have to give it up. We are fighting this war not to maintain, but to restore peace. In war more than ever, one must use what one is defending.

Article 25

Nothing is too valuable to be sacrificed for freedom. All we possess we won as a free people. Without our freedom, it would have no purpose, meaning or endurance. It is better for a nation to be impoverished but free rather than to seem prosperous, but end a war as slaves. A free people can rebuild everything it lost in defending its freedom. An enslaved people will lose that which survived the war, and also the ability to gain it back again.

Article 26

The duty of the individual during war extends to sacrificing his life for the life of his nation. In view of such great and final sacrifice, surely one must demand that each be ready to give up his goods and property if that is necessary for victory and the security of his nation! Only such willingness to sacrifice transforms a collection of individuals into a people, and in a higher sense, a nation.

Article 27

The goal of our government and military leadership is a German nation that can live freely in all important areas. Our generation must secure this through battle and hard work. It cannot be postponed until later. Either we do it, or it will never be done.

Article 28

Our generation has not only particular burdens, but also particular honor. If we win, and we can and must win, we will be the most famous generation in the history of Germany. If we lose, our names will be cursed through the centuries by the generations that must bear the frightful cost of our failure.

Article 29

There are people who have little interest in such matters. They are materialists who think only of comfort and pleasure, and who have no sense of their historic responsibilities. One can only hold them in contempt. They are ready to give up our nation's future for the pleasures of the moment. Wherever they speak, they must be dealt with firmly. They do not understand reason, only self-interest. They act under the principle: After us the deluge! Our reply to these unprincipled people is this: Even if we have to give up our dreams for many years, at least our children and grandchildren will have things better!

Article 30

Remember in all that you do and do not do, in all that you say and do not say, that you are a German! Believe loyally and unshakably in the Führer and in victory. Remember always that you are a child of the bravest and most industrious people on earth. We must suffer much to reach our goal, but the goal will be reached despite everything if only we hold true to all our virtues and are ready, if necessary to sacrifice everything in this war to guarantee the nation's freedom and its future.

Source: "Die 30 Kriegsartikel für das deutsche Volk," Der steile Aufstieg (Munich: Zentralverlag der NSDAP, 1944), 464–474. Copyright © 1999 by Randall Bytwerk. Reprinted with permission.

Analysis

By the end of September 1943, the situation for Germany looked bleak indeed. Stalingrad had represented a huge blow to German prestige (See Document 14); and during September, British planes alone had dropped 14,000 tons of bombs on German cities. On September 3, Allied troops had landed on the

Italian mainland and on the same day the Badoglio government had signed an armistice with them. The propaganda minister had persuaded a reluctant Hitler to broadcast to the German people on September 10. The speech was largely confined to accusing Badoglio of treachery and praising Mussolini. But Goebbels was satisfied with the favorable feedback of the speech. Nevertheless, his diary entries for September (see in particular, entries of September 9 and 25), Goebbels indicates that he remains worried about the morale of the people and that these "dos' and don'ts" of the (eventual) "Thirty Articles" of war were intended to guide them. His diary entry (see also entry for September 25) also reveals that it was intended as a sort of "manifesto" to be issued as a pamphlet and circulated widely. Fanatical belief and an unbridled pride in the nation are the order of the day.

The keynote of the appeal is struck in Article 1: "Everything may be possible in this war except one thing: that we should ever capitulate or bow to the force of the enemy. Those who spoke or even only thought of it were traitors and must be expelled from the fighting and working German community in utter disgrace."

The defensive character of the war (*Verteidigungskrieg*) on the usual Nazi lines was stressed in Article 3: "It has been imposed upon us by our enemies in order to cut off any national chances of living and developing." A lost war would mean that the present generation of Germans had gambled away the achievements of preceding generations. The people must trust the government (even when silent) and must make every effort to integrate themselves and to let their deeds and thoughts be fed by the deepest sense of community from which the duties of the individual German in wartime derive.

Article 11 refers to the impact of enemy propaganda "which attempts an old trick of political warfare to separate a people from its Government, in order to deprive it of its leadership and to make it defenceless." The possible success of this trick would be the only means by which the enemy could overcome Germany. Those who fell prey to this ruse were branded blockheads or traitors and severe penalties were threatened against them. Other types denounced in more or less strong terms were the "know-alls" ('*Sie sind zwar Besserwisser, aber keineswegs Besserkönner*'—Article 12), the thoughtless or careless talkers (Article 13), who often forgot that the enemy was listening, the war parasites who took no interest in the war effort (Article 19) and the amusement mob, who thought only of their creature comforts and lacked all historical sense (Article 29). Significantly, Goebbels also attacked "the stupid phrase" that the leaders (*Leitung*) led a better life than the people. However, heavy the material losses of some individuals might be, they could not be compared with the very heavy burden of responsibility carried by the leadership and involving never-ending worries (Article 18).

Goebbels justified his attacks on non-conformists at home with the need to be worthy of the soldiers at the front. Those who died at the front fulfilling their duties could "demand that persons who sabotage or endanger the war at home should suffer death" (Article 21).

The sacrifices demanded are to be made for freedom. As was seen earlier, it was not individual freedom but national freedom, which Goebbels propagated with rationalizations of the existing situation such as "It is better for a nation to come out of a war very poor but free than seemingly in full control of its property but 'unfree'" (Article 25).

Goebbels used the argument of the better life to be enjoyed by future generations to justify sacrifices in war: "If we have to renounce happiness for many years, at least our children and grandchildren will have a better life" (Article 29).

Finally, Article 30 reminded the people of their duties to the fatherland and Führer and the superiority of the "chosen people": "In everything you do and omit to do, you say and keep silent about, bear in mind that you are a German. Believe loyally and unshakeably in the Führer and in victory! Remember always that you are a child of the bravest and most industrious people on earth, a people that has to bear much adversity and suffering to reach its goal. . . . in order to safeguard its freedom and its future" (Article 30).

In the final year of the war, belief in final victory continued to figure prominently in Nazi propaganda; there was no mention or suggestion of surrender. However, Hitler's absence from the bombed cities was widely commented on in the intelligence reports (See Document 30). And yet a few days before Hitler and Goebbels were both to commit suicide, the Führer's presence in Berlin was still apparently delaying the end of the war. Slogans, such as "Where the Führer is—victory is!," were a continuing expression of defiance. In April 1945, with the Russians encircling Berlin, the Ministry for Popular Enlightenment and Propaganda was disbanded. It must be said, however, why so many Germans fought to the bitter end in 1945 were only partly to do with propaganda. When all other methods of persuasion had failed, the Nazis had, for some time, resorted to fear and terror from the Werwolf organization, as an antidote to cowardice.[2] A more likely explanation for the limited success enjoyed by Goebbels during the final period of fighting lies in a traditional German patriotism and respect for authority, together with a fear of Bolshevism, which led people to defend their country intuitively. This sense of resignation has been described most aptly by one historian Helmut Krausnick, as one of "reluctant loyalty."[3]

Notes

1. A. Rhodes, *Propaganda. The Art of Persuasion: World War II* (Leicester: Magna Books, 1993), 217. In 1943, a United Nations Stamp was issued consisting of portraits of Roosevelt, Churchill, Stalin, and Chiang Kai-Shek with the slogan: "Victory through Unity."

2. The name given to a resistance force created by the Nazis in the final phase of the war to operate behind enemy lines as the Allies advanced through Germany. The organization operated through intimidation and fear but only played a significant role in the last months of the war.

3. Cf. H. Krausnick et al., *The Anatomy of the SS State* (London: Collins, 1968). For the propaganda impact in Nazi Germany during wartime see, D. Welch, *The Third Reich. Politics and Propaganda* (London: Routledge, 2002), 117–156.

Chapter 15

Feedback Agencies:
Gauging Propaganda Success

How do we measure "successful" propaganda? It is a recurring issue, and as the
scale of mass communications has proliferated, so have the means by which
governments have attempted to measure public opinion. The historian A.J.P.
Taylor once famously said, in the context of World War I, that you "cannot
conduct a gallup poll amongst the dead." Nevertheless, even during the Great
War, most governments did possess some limited feedback on public opinion
by means of police reports and letters to newspapers and magazines. But mea-
suring public opinion was still in its infancy.

During the interwar period, totalitarian fascist and communist states not
only monopolized the means of communication but also established agencies to
monitor closely both public reaction to their policies and factors affecting public morale. This process operated largely in "closed" societies away from foreign
opinion and influences. It may surprise some people to learn that Goebbels
impressed on all his staff at the Propaganda Ministry the imperative necessity
of constantly gauging the public mood. He, therefore, regularly received (as did
all the Nazi elite) extraordinarily detailed reports (*SD Berichte*) about this from
the secret police of the Nazi Security Service (*Sicherheitsdienst*).

At the outbreak of World War II, all the major belligerents had in place
organizations providing detailed information on popular attitudes. In Britain,
Mass Observation (MO) worked for the Ministry of Information (MOI), which
also used the Home Intelligence Reports, and in the United States, the Office of
Government Reports (OGR) provided "opinions, desires and complaints of the
citizens" for the Office of War Information (OWI).

Although the MOI had been reestablished relatively early in the war, it had no
coordinated system of intelligence on what the British public was actually thinking and feeling about the war and its impact. It quickly discovered an alarming
gulf between government and governed, which was exemplified in one of its
first posters—"*Your* courage, *Your* Cheerfulness, *Your* Resolution WILL BRING
US VICTORY"—which was widely criticized for its patronizing tone. The MOI
responded by setting up its Home Intelligence Division in January 1940.[1] In
addition, it started a program of wartime social surveys, the investigators being
labeled by the public as "Cooper's Snoopers," after Duff Cooper, minister for
information between May 1940 and July 1941. The Home Intelligence Reports
were compiled every week between 1940 and 1944. They were drawn up on the
basis of weekly submissions compiled from 13 regional offices to help guide the

MOI in its work by presenting "an unbiased and objective picture of the state of British public opinion on matters connected with the war" and to assess "as accurately as possible, the general state of public confidence."[2] When victory appeared certain at the end of 1944, the reports were discontinued.

The ministry also had access to the information provided by the BBC's Listener Research Department, which recorded the reaction of the public to news and other programs broadcast by the corporation. Further information was provided by Mass Observation, which had been founded in 1937, in order to study British society. Mass Observation was a fact-finding body that recruited a team of observers and a panel of volunteer writers to study the everyday lives of ordinary people in Britain and was commissioned by the MOI to carry out survey on British public opinion on specific issues.

World War II brought about dramatic development in the U.S. government's use of propaganda. The government created new agencies to make propaganda an acceptable way of interpreting information. The United States was the only major power that did not have an established government propaganda agency when the war broke out. In response to this, President Roosevelt created the Office of Government Reports (OGR) in 1939. Referred to as "OGRE" by its critics, OGR's head was Lowell Mellet, former editor of the *Washington Daily News*, now a presidential assistant. According to Clayton Koppes and Gregory Black, OGR "disseminated accurate, neutral information, while withholding adverse news. This information was placed in a context designed to build public confidence about America's growing military power." With this agency in place, the government began slowly to influence the available information available to the public. OGR accomplished this by "serving as a clearing house for information about the defense program . . . [and] informing the executive branch about public opinion,"[3] allowing for a bolder agency to be established in 1940—the Office of Facts and Figures (OFF). Roosevelt created the Office of Facts and Figures to consolidate smaller agencies and into one organization focused on providing informational propaganda and the Office of the Coordinator of Information (OCI), a new covert intelligence agency that included a propaganda branch. In the summer of 1942, the U.S. government regrouped its various propaganda agencies into a single Office of War Information (OWI), although some psychological operations remained under the new Office of Strategic Services (OSS).[4]

Document 30

HOME INTELLIGENCE REPORT FOR SEPTEMBER 11 AND 12, 1940

Document

Wednesday 11 September 1940

Reports now received make it possible to assess critically the effects of continued bombing in the East End. Morale is rather more strained than the newspapers suggest, whereas the damage to property seems to be less than is reported by them. The pictures of devastation and accounts of destruction weaken the resolve of people to stay put.

Organized evacuation is necessarily a slow business but is proceeding uninterruptedly. Voluntary evacuation also continues fairly steadily, though there is a tendency for those who work in badly-affected districts to evacuate themselves during the night and to return in the daytime.

Factors which contribute to the strain on morale are, of course, as much psychological as material. Listening tension (e.g. anticipation of planes and bombs) is one to which little official notice has been paid. Few people are using ear pads or understand that the diminution of noise can do much to lessen their state of anxiety. Nor does there seem to have been enough encouragement for people to try and sleep as and when they can. The fear, mostly among men, that they may lose their jobs, as has already happened in many cases in the Silvertown district, is an added anxiety, and if it were possible for some reassurance to be given that speedy efforts will be made to find other work for them this would undoubtedly have a good effect.

The need for mobile canteens is still urgent, as is the necessity for providing a hot meal every day for families evacuated from their homes.

An increase is reported in the number of people listening to Haw-Haw and rumours, mostly exaggerated accounts of raid damage and casualties have also increased considerably.

A certain amount of anti-Semitism in the East End still persists, but this is not so much on account of a marked difference in conduct between Jews and Cockneys, but because the latter, seeking a scapegoat as an outlet for emotional disturbances, pick on the traditional and nearest one. Though many Jewish people regularly congregate and sleep in the public shelters, so also do many of the Gentiles, nor is there any evidence to show that one or other predominates among those who have evacuated themselves voluntarily through fear or hysteria.

Reports from the Regions show that their attention is directed mainly towards London's sufferings and consequently their own troubles are to some extent diminished. Shelter problems are common to many districts as are also the various types and causes of anxiety associated with raids. There is, however, no sign of morale weakening, or that powers of resistance and determination are deteriorating.

Thursday 12 September 1940

In London particularly morale is high: people are much more cheerful today.

The dominating topic of conversation today is the anti-aircraft barrage of last night. This greatly stimulated morale: in public shelters people cheered and conversation shows that the noise brought a shock of positive pleasure. It made people feel that "all the time we had a wonderful trick up our sleeves ready to play when the moment came."

The increased noise kept people awake but tiredness is offset by the stimulus which has been created.

The Prime Minister's speech was well received but not so enthusiastically as usual. The speech was admired for its plain speaking, but there is evidence that many people, having convinced themselves that invasion is "off," disliked being reminded of it again. Some people remarked that he sounded "tired." In Wales people were surprised that Wales was omitted as a possible point of invasion. The speech nowhere created alarm.

There is still a good deal of unplanned evacuation from London, and there is evidence that small batches of refugees arriving without money at provincial stations are creating anxiety and some alarm. There are exaggerated stories of the damage to London circulating in the provinces. These reports are partly due to the stories told by these refugees, but there is also evidence that Haw-Haw rumours have greatly increased.

A reliable observer just returned to London from the North reports that press and radio have given an account of London damage which has an exaggerated effect. Many people appear to think that London is "in flames." There is great sympathy for London and on the whole a belief that "London will see it through."

Source: U.K. National Archives, INF 1/290, "The Work of the Home Intelligence Division 1939–1944." Contains public sector information licensed under the Open Government License v3.0.

Analysis

Document 30 is a Home Intelligence Report for September 11 and 12, 1940, following a major and sustained Luftwaffe attack on London. During the month of September, 6,600 died, of whom 5,500 were in the London area. The deficiencies of Civil Defense preparations were cruelly exposed during the first days of the London Blitz and the Home Intelligence Reports reflect some of the negative aspects of the experience behind the propaganda image portrayed in films such as *London Can Take It* of the ever-cheerful, resolute cockney. The introductory section, written by the director of Home Intelligence (Mary Adams), to every report, assessed the critical effects of continued bombing in the East End: "morale is rather more strained than the newspapers suggest." It was also noted that there was a discernible increase to the number of people listening to the Nazi propaganda broadcasts of Lord Haw-Haw (William Joyce) and the rumors he was spreading, mostly exaggerated accounts of air-raid damage and civilian casualties. Another sign of stress was the revival of anti-Jewish prejudices that Oswald Mosley and the British Union of Fascists had exploited in the 1930s. "A certain amount of anti-Semitism in the East End still persists, but this is not so much on account of a marked difference in conduct between Jews and Cockneys, but because the latter, seeking a scapegoat as an outlet for emotional disturbances, pick on the traditional and nearest one." Home Intelligence also reported on the growing fear of homelessness and unemployment due to the destruction. In London, both planned and unplanned evacuations were underway with varying degrees of success. The report also noted that Winston Churchill's speech broadcast on September 11 was well received "but not as enthusiastically as usual." Some interviewed remarked that the prime minister sounded "tired."

On the positive side, Home Intelligence recorded that morale received a boost on the night of September 11 when London's aircraft defenses, recently reinforced, blazed away at the Luftwaffe. When Buckingham Palace was also hit a few days later, this proved to be a propaganda coup for the MOI and for George VI and Queen Elizabeth, who were in residence at the time. Reports suggested that the King and Queen were "in the front line too" and the "way in which they freely visited the bombed areas is the subject of much favourable comment." A constant theme from these reports is that "we know what we are taking—what are we dishing out to the enemy?"[5]

Like Mass Observation, the Home Intelligence Reports contain a synthesis of peoples' concerns, fears, attitudes and opinions on all matters related to themselves and the wider events going on around them. However, what is important to remember is that these reports were "official" and informed the government on the state of the nation.

Document 31

SD REPORT: TO THE PARTY CHANCELLERY: "BASIC ISSUES CONCERNING THE MOOD AND BEHAVIOR OF THE GERMAN PEOPLE; TRUST IN THE LEADERSHIP" (NOVEMBER 29, 1943)

Document

The first serious shocks occurred with the reserves of the last two winters of the war in Russia. It was then that for the first time doubts emerged about whether the leadership was fully capable of grasping the enormous problems created by the war and mastering them. In the course of this year's developments the question had been raised more frequently . . .

In such deliberations the population makes a clear *distinction between the Führer and other leading figures.* Whereas loss of trust in individual leading personalities or leading agencies occurs comparatively frequently, faith in the Führer is virtually unshaken. While it has certainly been subjected to various serious stresses, particularly after Stalingrad, recent months have revealed a strengthening of trust in the Führer. Recently it reached a high point with the *freeing of Mussolini and the Führer speech* on the night of 9 November. "Here the German people believed they were seeing the Führer again in all his greatness." . . . Many people see in the Führer the only guarantee of a successful conclusion of the war. The idea that anything could happen to the Führer is unthinkable.

Thus, while the Führer is the only person who is considered capable of mastering the present situation, the remaining leadership of the Reich is no longer trusted unconditionally. In particular, the failure of promises and prophecies to be fulfilled has seriously undermined trust in individual leaders as far as many compatriots are concerned.

Above all there is a marked loss of trust in the media. The attempt from time to time to disguise the true picture when the situation was serious or to play down ominous military developments, for example "by portraying withdrawal as a success" or "presenting territory which previously had been described as valuable as now being not so important at all" or "thinking that periods of delay have to be filled with flannel-type reports about events in India or plutocratic excesses in England or America," have largely undermined trust in the press and radio which previously existed.

Thus in their desire for objectivity and openness and their dislike of attempts to portray things as better than they are the population has gradually begun to read between the lines and, in particular, increasingly to turn to the news from neutral and enemy states.

A further cause for mistrust in the leadership is the behavior of individual local leading figures in the State and Party at lower and middle levels. Although the measures of the Reich Government are generally approved of, much of what they see being done by the executive organs of the State and Party gives compatriots cause for concern. For example the population note that barter and illicit trading keep spreading or that the "total war" propagated by the leadership is not being fairly implemented (eg. In the case of the deployment of women, the question of housemaids, the allocation of housing and, above all, the granting of reserved worker status) and that some of the leading figures are not affected by the restrictions which are imposed on everyone else . . . This has led many to believe that the leadership does not always share in the nation's sacrifices. There are "double standards" and they "preach water but drink wine.' Poor behavior by individual persons in authority often damaged trust in the top leadership at the local level.

Workers' trust in the leadership of their plants, in the DAF (German Labour Front) and other organizations is often subject to particular strain. Many workers are once more beginning to *think in terms of classes* and talk of classes who would "exploit" them.

As far as the Werhmacht is concerned, the population is convinced of the professional and personal qualities of the German military leadership . . . However, the excesses in the bases and to some extent in the home garrisons have been the subject of growing criticism . . . Reference is made to the alleged growing gap between the officers and men among troops behind the front and at home . . .

To sum up, the report reveals the following:

1. The population makes *a distinction between the Führer and the rest of the leadership* in its assessment of professional performance and personal behavior.

2. The criticism of individual leading figures and of measures ordered by the leading agencies, which in some cases comes not from opponents or the usual complainers, but from wide circles of the population, indicates a certain reduction in trust in the leadership.

3. *Fairness and the equal distribution of the burdens of war will determine the degree of trust in the leadership.* The trust is undermined above all if measures are not applied equally or totally and when exceptions are made and when there are "back doors" and when action is not taken irrespective of the person affected.

Source: Jeremy Noakes (ed.), Nazism, 1919–1945, vol. 4: The German Home Front in World War II (Exeter: University of Exeter Press, 1998), 550–551.

Analysis

Document 31 is an example of how the Nazis attempted to monitor public opinion during a key moment in the war following the fall of Stalingrad. In recent years, a number of key sources have been exploited more fully in an attempt to understand the Nazi regime's problems of political control and mobilization. The first is the various reports on civilian morale and public opinion conducted from 1939 by the Security Service (*Sichereitsdienst* or SD) of the *Schuzstaffel* (SS) and later, under cover, by the RMVP (propaganda ministry) itself.[6] Their reports were based on information received from agents throughout the Reich, which reported on their conversations with party members or on conversation they overheard. It has been estimated that by 1939, the SD had some 3,000 full-time officials and some 50,000 part-time agents.[7]

The morale of the German people continued to deteriorate throughout the summer of 1943. The fall of Mussolini on July 27, 1943, had shaken German public opinion. Although Goebbels had responded with his "Thirty Articles of War" (See Document 29), by November an important factor in the decline of popular morale was the growing contempt for much of its leadership. Document 31 is taken from a special report from the SD to the Party Chancellery and is dated November 23, 1943. The report suggests that, while faith in Hitler remained generally strong, the rest of the Nazi leadership was no longer trusted unconditionally. The freeing of Mussolini and Hitler's radio broadcast on November 9 is cited as a key factor: "Here the German people believed that they were seeing the Führer again in all his greatness." Revealingly, the report also detected a marked loss of trust in the German media and called for greater objectivity and openness. As a result, the population increasingly "turn to the news from neutral and enemy states." This is something that Allied intelligence picked up on, and by employing "black" clandestine radio stations and leaflet drops, attempted to drive a wedge between the Nazi leadership and the ordinary German citizen who was experiencing incremental hardships due to the changing nature of the military situation.[8]

Overall, the report suggest a widening gulf between the "ordinary" citizen and local party leaders, and it represents a devastating critique of the failure of the Reich leadership to convince the population that sacrifices were being shared equally. This perception (whether real or imagined) represented a real challenge for Goebbels and Nazi propaganda in the final stage of the war.

Both the SD report and the Home Intelligence Reports provide revealing insights into two different political cultures experiencing "total war." Both have limitations; they are not "scientific" in terms of their scope and sophistication when compared to contemporary social surveys. We need to recognize that they were "impressionistic" in that the people interviewed, like the compilers of the reports, did not know what was going to happen next and were reacting to events without any of the historical perspective that we now possess. Nevertheless, they offer the best possible evidence of how ordinary people responded to official propaganda disseminated by governments and as such, they provide historians with some idea of what it must have been like to have lived through a period of cataclysmic developments.

Notes

1. The poster drew the following comment from the *Times*: "The insipid and patronizing invocations to which the passer-by is now being treated have a power of exasperation which is all their own." Quoted in I. McLaine, *Ministry of Morale. Home Front Morale and the Ministry of Information in World War II* (London: George Allen & Unwin, 1979), 86. For examples of the Home Intelligence Reports see, P. Addison and J. Crang (eds.), *Listening to Britain: Home Intelligence Reports on Britain's Finest Hours* (London: Vintage, 2011).

2. Cited in, *Persuading the People* (London: HMSO, 1995), 10.

3. C. R. Koppes and G. D. Black, *Hollywood Goes to War. How Politics, Profit and Propaganda Shaped World War II Movies* (Oakland: University of California Press, 1987), 51.

4. For the most comprehensive account of OWI's activities see, A. M. Winkler, *The Politics of Propaganda: The Office of War Information, 1942–1945* (New Haven, CT: Yale University Press, 1978).

5. The MOI were aware of this feeling—especially in the urban conurbations that were experiencing constant air attacks. In 1942, it commissioned the documentary film *Target for Tonight*, directed by Harry Watt that showed RAF attacks on German cities. It proved highly popular with British cinema audience and the film went on to win an honorary Academy Award in 1942 and "Best Documentary" by National Board of Review in 1941.

6. The other key source is the *Deutschland-Berichte* (Sopade), underground reports from the Social Democratic Party's contacts, both those stationed in Germany and those travelling through it from outside, who passed on their observations in the form of lengthy monthly reports to the SPD headquarters in exile These reports cover the period of 1934–1940 and are, therefore, largely outside the scope of this study. Although the Sopade reports, together with the SD reports, have their drawbacks and must be used critically, nevertheless, they have greatly contributed to our understanding of the popular base of Nazism and to the ongoing debate about the "power" or otherwise of Nazi propaganda.

7. See D. Welch, *The Third Reich. Politics and Propaganda* (London: Routledge, 2002), 117–144.

8. One of the British black radio stations, *G3 Gustav Siegfried Eins (GS1)*, undertook detail feedback on the success (or otherwise) its propaganda broadcasts. The monitoring transcripts can be found on the excellent Psycwar.org website, sample reference: http://www.psywar.org/delmer/8251/1649.

Chapter 16

Witness to War

Together with official feedback agencies that were set up by belligerent government to monitor its own propaganda and that of its enemies, the historian also has access to the private diaries kept by people from all walks of life. These may also shed light on reactions to official propaganda. Document 1 set out the establishment and principles that underpinned the Ministry of Information in 1939. The new ministry was not an immediate success, especially during the so-called phoney war when there was no fighting on the Western Front (Cf. Document 3). Changes, however, were taking place on the domestic front, where the British government was planning for total war by centralizing control of much of British society. This included strict censorship. According to one American journalist working in London, Quentin Reynolds, censorship at the time was "petty, absurd, tyrannical."[1]

The MOI was established initially to handle certain tasks—the release of official news; security censorship of the press, films, and the BBC; the maintenance of morale; and the conduct of publicity campaigns for government departments. The structure and multiplicity of functions bemused outside observers and the first minister of information, Lord Macmillan, in an extraordinary moment of candor, confessed to the House of Lords, "I may say that I have had considerable difficulty in ascertaining what *are* (my italics) its function."[2] In an internal memo penned in September 1939, shortly after its establishment, the MOI noted "with some alarm that . . . The public is stolidly facing a catastrophe. There is a danger that this attitude may degenerate into defeatism."

These views, which were not made public at the time, are reinforced by the diary of Mollie Panter-Downes, a journalist for the *New Yorker*. In her entry of October 1, 1939, she writes about a "war of nerves" degenerating into a "war of yawns," due largely to the failures of the MOI.

Document 32

MOLLIE PANTER-DOWNES, DIARY ENTRY (OCTOBER 1, 1939)

Document

Criticism is in the air these days, after pretty nearly a month of the curious twenty-five-per-cent warfare. Everyone is slightly fed up with something or other; with the Ministry of Information, which doesn't inform; with the British Broadcasting Corporation, which accused of being depressing and—worse— boring; with the deficiencies of the fish supply, which have made fishmongers hoard herrings for their regular customers as though they were nuggets; and even with the bombs which don't drop. The war of nerves has degenerated into a war of yawns for thousands of Air Raid Protection workers, who spend their nights playing cards, taking cat naps, and practically yearning for a short, sharp air raid. The fact that many of them are drawing an average of £2 10s a week for doing nothing much accept waiting around has also caused a good deal of murmuring.

The Ministry of Information comes off worst with everybody. The man in the street feels, rather naturally, that he is paying plenty for this war, that he is entitled to know what is happening, and that he wants more to happen. He feels that something is rotten in a system which recently went through the most complicated acrobatics of releasing, suppressing, and releasing again, even such a harmless piece of news as Her Majesty's return to London from a visit to the Princesses at Balmoral. The Englishman grumbles, but to be long on patience is one of the traditional strengths of the British.

Source: W. Shawn (ed.), *Mollie Panter-Downes: London War Notes* (New York: Farrar, Strauss and Giroux, 1971), 14–15.

Analysis

Although this diary entry written during the phoney war is not an "official" account of morale in London, it nonetheless provides the historian with an informed observation written by a British journalist for a sympathetic America readership in the early stages of the war against Nazi Germany.[3] What emerges from this brief entry is the banality of the quotidian lives of (in this case) Londoners and the trivial things that concern and happen to ordinary people who have been placed in an extraordinary situation. The mundanity and yearning for something to happen during the phoney war is beautifully observed and, arguably, has never been so succinctly captured ("the war of nerves has degenerated into a war of yawns . . ."). The concentration on the personal and the particular is well suited to the magnifying lens of these despatches, which by their very shortness, draws the reader's attention to detail.

Mollie Panter-Downes's entry, written just a few months after the establishment of the MOI, confirms that the British government from the outset of the war showed a misplaced lack of confidence in the British people that continued until after the retreat at Dunkirk. The situation would, however, improve in July 1941, when Brendon Bracken took control of the ministry (with Churchill's moral support) and the MOI tapped into the "Dunkirk spirit." Panter-Downes's diary entry provides a journalistic insight into the mind of both the government and people during the period of the "phoney war."

Anti-Jewish propaganda was a central plank in the dissemination of the Nazi *Weltanschauung* ("worldview"). In 1940, for example, three major anti-Semitic films were released—*Die Rothschilds* (The Rothschilds), *Jud Süss* (Jew Süss), and *Der ewige Jude* (The Eternal—or Wandering—Jew) to justify Nazi measures to convince the German people that a Jewish Question did exist, which needed to be "solved" (Cf. Document 44). The Nazi Propaganda Ministry gauged the impact of this so-called commercial film by means of its secret police reports. According to the SD report of November 28, 1940, "*Jud Süss* continues to receive an extraordinary favourable response." In December 1942, a 16-year-old Dutch Jewish boy, who had fled to Belgium, saw *Jud Süss* in a Brussels cinema. He recorded his impressions of the film in his diary.

Document 33

MOSHE FLINKER, DIARY ENTRY (DECEMBER 14, 1942)

Document

Yesterday I went to the movies with my sister. When I was still in The Hague, before it was occupied by the Germans, I didn't go to the cinema much. After the Germans had been in Holland for some time, they forbade the Jews to go to the cinema. Then they began showing anti-Semitic films. I wanted very much to see these movies, but I didn't dare, because my identity card was stamped "J" for Jew, and I could have been asked to show my papers at any time, and for such an offence I could have been sentenced to six months' imprisonment. But here, in Belgium, where I am not registered as a Jew, I can go to the movies. In any case, there is not the same strictness here. When we arrived, only the anti-Semitic cinema proprietors had notices posted in front denying entrance to Jews. Now, however, in front of every theatre is posted: "By order of the Germans, entrance to Jews is forbidden." Even so I went to see the film "Jew Süss." What I saw there made my blood boil. I was red in the face when I came out. I realized there the wicked objectives of these evil people—how they want to inject the poison of anti-Semitism into the blood of the gentiles. While I was watching the film I suddenly remembered what the evil one [Hitler] had said in one of his spectacles: "Whichever side wins the war, anti-Semitism will spread and spread until the Jews are no more." In that film I saw the means he is using to achieve his aim. And if nothing happens to counteract his work, then surely the poison will spread in people's blood. The way in which jealousy, hatred and loathing are aroused is simply indescribable . . .

Source: Young Moshe's Diary, *Yad Vashem* (Jerusalem, 1971), 42–43 (http://www.yadvashem.org/odot_pdf/Microsoft%20Word%20-%203814.pdf).

Analysis

Flinker's comments are particularly sensitive for it is a rare example of a contemporary Jewish reaction to a virulently anti-Semitic propaganda film made during the war period. It is striking that while he was living in Holland—and now in occupied Belgium—Jews were banned from attending the cinema at the risk of a six-month prison sentence. This statement, casually mentioned in the diary, illustrates the incremental nature of the Nazi persecution of Jews that led ultimately to the Holocaust. The second point to be made is that the film was still be shown in occupied territories two years after its initial release in Germany. Moshe Flinker's incandescent fury at the distorted claims made against Jews in the film is so intense that he is unable to fully articulate his feelings.[4] Nevertheless, for a frightened 16 year old, his fears are prescient; he cites Hitler's "evil" speech, which is a reference to Hitler "prophecy" speech to the Reichstag on January 30, 1939: "Should the international Jewish financiers succeed once again in plunging the nations into a world war, the result will not be the victory of Jews but the annihilation of the Jewish race in Europe." The speech was also shown at the end of the film *Der ewige Jude*. Flinker recognizes the power of the propaganda message in reinforcing already held prejudices against Jews and concluded that unless there is a "miracle from above" the Jews are "doomed." Tragically, no such miracle came to save Jews as the Third Reich implemented genocide, under the cloak of war, of unparalleled scope and brutality.[5]

Historians need to analyze diaries with a certain detachment and skepticism. Nevertheless, they remain an importance historical source. Private diaries written during World War II provide historians with the thoughts and insights of individuals caught up in a global conflict. Sometimes, they are written specifically for posterity by important historical figures (the diaries of Joseph Goebbels spring to mind); other diaries often were written by "ordinary" citizens engaged in chronicling their individual responses to momentous events. As such, they represent an important corrective source of what has been termed the "voice from below." Diaries written in times of conflict and chaos provide both a personal interpretation and invariably capture the immediacy of events that official documents can often fail to convey.

Notes

1. Q. Reynolds, *Only the Stars Are Neutral* (Sidney: Halstead Press, 1942), 142.

2. Quoted in I. McLaine, *Ministry of Morale. Home Front Morale and the Ministry of Information in World War II* (London: George Allen & Unwin, 1979), 39–40.

3. Mollie Panter-Downes began writing for the *New Yorker*, first a series of short stories, and from September 1939, a column titled "Letter from London," which she wrote until 1984. The collected columns were later published as *Letters from England* (1940) and *London War Notes* (1972).

4. The film is set in Württemberg in 1733, where the Jew Süss is appointed finance minister and he extols taxes from the poor citizens of the Duchy. Süss becomes so powerful that he eventually abducts and rapes, while her fiancé is tortured. Distracted with shame, the girl commits suicide. Süss is arrested and condemned to death by hanging. The father of the girl announces that all Jews must leave the city and hopes that "this lesson will never be forgotten." For a detailed analysis of this and other anti-Jewish films see, D. Welch, *Propaganda and the German Cinema, 1933–1945* (London: I.B. Tauris, 2001), 236–255.

5. Moshe Flinker and his family fled to Brussels in 1942. In 1944, the family was denounced by a fellow Jew and was transported to Auschwitz. Moshe and his parents died but his brother and sisters survived. After the war, they returned to their apartment in Brussels and found the diary that Moshe had been keeping in 1942. Information and citation from the diary from R. J. Aldrich, *Witness to War. Diaries of the Second World War in Europe and the Middle East* (London: Doubleday, 2004), 373–374.

Chapter 17

Animated Film and Sheet Music

During World War II, the United States also employed humor, notably through the Walt Disney studios and its popular animated icons such as Donald Duck, in order to symbolize true American values. The film *Der Führer's Face* (1943) was produced to support the American war-bond drive and to improve worker's efficiency on the home front. The film was directed by Jack Kinney and written by Joe Grant and Dick Huemer from the original music by Oliver Wallace. The film is well known for Wallace's original song "Der Führer's Face" (also known informally as "The Nazi Song"), which was released earlier by Spike Jones and His City Slickers.

The song parodied the Nazi anthem, the "Horst Wessel Lied."[1] Unlike the version in the cartoon, some Spike Jones versions contain the rude sound effect of an instrument he called the "birdaphone," a rubber razzer (sometimes referred to as the "Bronx Cheer") with each "Heil!" to show contempt for Hitler. (The version in the cartoon features the use of a tuba instead.) The so-called Bronx Cheer was a well-known expression of disgust in that time and was not deemed obscene or offensive. The sheet music cover bears the image of a tomato splattering in Hitler's face. In the Jones version, the chorus' line, "Ja, we is the Supermen" is answered by a soloist's "Super-duper super men!" delivered in an effeminate character that was intended to undermine the Nazi's image of themselves as a super-masculine warrior soldiers. It is another example of using humor to reduce a frightening enemy to the level of visibility and ridicule (Charles Ridley used a similar technique in his 1941 British film, *Germany Calling*). The recording became one of the biggest hits during World War II.

Der Führer's Face depicted in simplistic terms what life was like for someone living in the Third Reich, namely, swastika wallpaper, even swastika-shaped trees, substitute coffee and regimentalized work without holidays for the glorification of the Führer. Its opening song, played by a strutting Nazi "oompah" band (though also with a Japanese bandsman, for good measure), slyly mixes subservience with insult: "When der Führer says, 'We ist der master race'/We Heil! Heil! Right in der Führer's Face." Fortunately, the oppression of life under Nazi rule is just a nightmarish dream. In the final scene, Donald awakes to see a shadow on his bedroom wall that turns out to be a replica of the Statue of Liberty—revealing in symbolic terms why the American people are fighting the war. Donald embraces the statue, proud that he is an American citizen. The film ends with a caricature of Hitler's angry face followed by a few "Heils" and

Donald throwing a tomato on the Führer's face in typical vaudeville tradition. On impact, the tomato forms the words "The End."

Throughout the film, Disney contrasts the "free" and "slave world" of democracy and Nazism. Such contrasts, which are simplistic and disseminated in crude black and white terms, were first used in Frank Capra's *Why We Fight* series of documentary films (1942–1945) (see Document 4). *Der Führer's Face* won the Academy Award for best Animated Short Film at the 15th Academy Awards in 1943. It was the only *Donald Duck* film to receive the honor.

Note

1. Horst Ludwig Wessel (October 9, 1907-February 23, 1930) was a German Nazi party activist and an SA-Sturmführer who was made a martyr of the Nazi movement following his violent death in 1930. He was the author of the lyrics to the song "Die Fahne hoch" ("*The Flag on High*"), usually known as "Horst Wessel Lied," which became the Nazi Party anthem and, *de facto*, Germany's co-national anthem from 1933 to 1945.

Chapter 18

Art and War

The strict regulation of the art world under various totalitarian regimes was unprecedented in the annals of art history and represented the high point of the appropriation of art as propaganda. For the totalitarian dictatorships of Germany, Italy, Japan, and the Soviet Union, World War II did not really change policy radically. Art had for some years served the political purposes of totalitarian masters; in such regimes, art and culture had been mobilized from the outset in the service of the state—to different degrees and for different purposes. So, the main difference between the war art of the totalitarian and democratic countries is, arguably, one of function.

Britain's World War II art program went out of its way to encourage the painting of nonviolent, sentimental, and rather parochial scenes of Britons "doing their bit," intended to inspire people to protect their countryside and ways of life. As most artists supported the war aims, they tended to shy away from the confrontational. In World War II, advances in war technology, and particularly the emergence of the bomber, served to transform the experience of civilians fighting under the new conditions of total war. The home front attracted, not surprisingly, major artists and significant commissions and arguably the most memorable art of the war *was* done on the Home Front, even though remarkable pictures were made of the overseas theaters of operations.

Kulturpolitik (cultural policy) was an important element in German life, but the Nazis were the first party to systematically organize the entire cultural life of a nation. The war was seen as a battle for the salvation of German culture and also served to heighten the major propaganda themes of the regime. In striking contrast to what happened during World War I, during the 1939–1945 conflict millions of Germans encountered deadly and destructive violence *within* Germany. Revealingly, the suffering of war is almost totally absent from art; artists were discouraged from recording how civilians coped with the pressure of Allied bombing raids on their cities. Such fortitude was not considered sufficiently "heroic"; instead, art was used to bolster the lie of a victorious Germany. Painters such as Elk Eber, Fritz Erler, Wilhelm Sauter, and Franz Eichhorst specialized in glorifying soldiers and victorious battles, as Nazi propaganda regularly suggested a continuity between World War I and World War II.

In Wilhelm Sauter's *The Eternal Soldier* (1940), the two are juxtaposed, suggesting that they are both part of the same struggle. In Hans Schmitz-Wiedenbrück's *Workers, Farmers and Soldiers,* (1941), all three pillars of the state are elevated to iconic status, conveying the National Socialist message of Aryan solidarity and heroic sacrifice.

Document 34

HANS SCHMITZ-WIEDENBRÜCK'S *WORKERS, FARMERS AND SOLDIERS* (1941)

Document

Source: Kunst im Deutschen Reich, August/September 1941. Courtesy of the German Propaganda Archive and Randall Bytwerk (http://www.bytwerk.com/gpa/naziwarart.htm).

Analysis

While the Nazis admired Greek art, their tightly proscribed cultural policy created bland, arrogant, bombastic works that now look like the stuff of kitsch cartoon fantasy comics—but totally drained of humor and irony; Hans Schmitz-Wiedenbrück's *Workers, Farmers and Soldiers* used the traditional format of the triptych to convey a Nazi message. The portrayal of the workers and farmers is particularly revealing. These are core Aryan stereotypes in Nazi propaganda and the work they are seen carrying out is intended to represent a world ennobled by muscular vitality, not one of exploitation and exhaustion. The idealized Aryan worker is a hero-figure making a major contribution to the German war effort. There is a notable absence of modern machinery that reflects the Nazi's essentially anti-modern message and the alienation they associated with modern industrial society. While the worker's represent two of the main pillars of the Nazi state, they are not equal. The three elements of the German armed forces (referred to in the painting's title as "soldiers") dominate the picture, not only by its central position in the triptych, but also because they are painted as if seen from below, a well-known artistic device to create awe and a sense of authority and power.

TOM LEA, *THE PRICE* (USA, 1944)

Document

Source: Oil on canvas, 36 × 28. Life Collection of Art WWII, US Army Center of Military History, Washington, DC.

Analysis

Document 35 is a rare study of death and destruction that is intended to bring home not the heroism of war but its gritty and devastating reality. In January 1943, George Biddle, a mural artist and the brother of the U.S. secretary general, was invited by the assistant secretary of war to form a War Department Art Advisory committee and serve as chair. The army, inspired by the success of a small war artist program in World War I, had been considering sending artists into battle since early 1942. Biddle's committee, which would be responsible for selecting the artists, included the noted artist Henry Varnum Poor, the director of the Metropolitan Museum of Art Francis Henry Taylor, and the writer John Steinbeck. Steinbeck was an active supporter of the war art program and wrote to Biddle: "It seems to me that a total war would require the use not only of all of the material resources of the nation but also the spiritual and psychological participation of the whole people. And the only psychic communication we have is through the arts."

A total of 42 army artists were eventually selected by the committee to work in 12 theaters of war around the world. In March 1943, they were sent a memorandum by Biddle outlining their mission:

> . . . Any subject is in order, if as artists you feel that it is part of War; battle scenes and the front line battle landscapes; the dying and the dead; prisoners of war; field hospitals and base hospitals; wrecked habitations and bombing scenes; character sketches of our own troops, of prisoners, of the natives of the countries you visit; never official portraits; the tactical implements of war; embarkation and debarkation scenes; the nobility, courage, cowardice, cruelty, boredom of war; all this should form part of a well-rounded picture. Try to omit nothing; duplicate to your heart's content. Express if you can, realistically or symbolically, the essence and spirit of war. You may be guided by Blake's mysticism, by Goya's cynicism and savagery, by Delacroix's romanticism, by Daumier's humanity and tenderness; or better still follow your own inevitable star. We believe that our Army Command is giving you an opportunity to bring back a record of great value to our country. Our committee wants to assist you to that end.

The artwork in question was painted by Tom Lea and titled, *The Price*. The artist created it while employed by *LIFE* magazine as a war artist in the Pacific theater of war. Lea was attached to a Marine unit that assaulted the Japanese-held island of Peleliu, and he was trained and equipped like every other Marine, except that he went into battle armed with a sketch pad and pens as his primary weapons. Lea had actually witnessed the soldier's death during the bloody landing, and he sketched the soldier's agony as it occurred. Back in the studio, Lea transformed his black and white pen sketch into an unforgettable oil painting. In the battle of Peleiu, the U.S. Marines suffered 1,121 killed in action, with over 6,000 casualties. All 10,000 Japanese soldiers holding the island were killed. Reporting for *LIFE* magazine on the story of the invasion, Lea would write of the brutal landing:

> Lying in terror looking longingly up the slope to better cover, I saw a wounded man near me, staggering in the direction of the LVTs. His face was half bloody

pulp and the mangled shreds of what was left of an arm hung down like a stick, as he bent over in the stumbling, shock-crazy walk. The half of his face that was still human had the most terrifying look of abject patience's I have ever seen. He fell behind me, in a red puddle on the white sand.

The painting is both shocking and almost surreal in its comic book sense of exaggeration. The mangled shreds of the blood-soaked arm are in stark contrast to the rest of the soldier's body and uniform which appears almost pristine. The soldier has been caught clearly unawares is reinforced by the fact that his rifle is still strapped over his back. He is not engaged for combat but has been mortally wounded, nonetheless. It is that sense of shock and helplessness that the artist has captured in the anguished face of the dying soldier. Lea's other major work from the Peleliu campaign, *That 2000 Yard Stare* (1944), proved equally powerful and disturbing to American audiences.[1]

Note

1. Material taken from B. M. Greeley Jr. (ed.), *The Two Thousand Yard Stare: Tom Lea's World War II* (Texas: A&M University Press, 2008).

Chapter 19

Propaganda under Occupation: Vichy France

Vichy France, officially the French State (*État français*), was the government of Marshal Philippe Pétain's regime during France's occupation by Nazi Germany in World War II. From 1940 to 1942, while nominally the government of France as a whole, Vichy only fully controlled the unoccupied zone in southern France, while Germany occupied northern and western France. When the Germans invaded France in May 1940, Pétain was still revered as a World War I hero, the victor of the battle of Verdun. Despite being 84 years old, he was made a vice premiere to Paul Reynaud to bolster national morale and in June, with German troops overrunning the country, he was put in charge. "I make France the gift of my person," he announced on the radio and asked the Germans for an armistice. They agreed and the French Senate and Chamber of Deputies, meeting in the spa town of Vichy with the Germans occupying two-thirds of France, unhesitatingly made Pétain chief of state (*Chef de l'État Français*).

Pétain formed an authoritarian government that remained implacably anti-republican and collaborated extensively with the Germans. He wanted to restore an old-fashioned respect for religion, patriotism, and the family. The motto of the Vichy regime was "Travail, Famille, Patrie" (Work, Family, Fatherland), which replaced the French revolutionary slogan "Liberté, Egalité, Fraternité" (Freedom, Equality, Brotherhood). The song, "Here We Are Marshal," was adopted and became the new Vichy anthem. The cover to the sheet music became a poster and showed a cross-section of the "new" France, with the flags of the Legion of ex-servicemen marching toward Pétain. The final verse was

The war is inhuman
What a sad horror
Let's not listen to hatred anymore let's exalt work
And let's retain confidence
In a new destiny
Because Pétain is France!
And France is Pétain

Vichy propaganda depicted Pétain as the father of the nation, a war-hero who would unify the nation. By identifying an authoritarian leader-figure with the nation, Vichy propaganda was disseminating a major ideological plank of fascist parties throughout Europe. Supporters of Vichy claimed that Pétain had no other choice but to seek an armistice and collaboration with Nazi Germany, and that his actions had brought an end to war and spared the French empire.

When Pétain became head of the *Etat Français* in 1940, an important propaganda drive was begun to reconcile the country to the difficult and humiliating position in which it found itself in the wake of the armistice, occupation, and in the climate of collaboration. Pétain's primary aims were to unite the country under his own leadership, to disseminate the principles of the *Révolution nationale*, and to promote a vision of the important role that France was to play in the New Europe. Youth was to play an essential part in this vision of a rejuvenated France—both as a metaphor for the lost innocence and simplicity of a country whose degeneracy and sophistication had led to the *débâcle* of defeat, and, in more practical terms, as the means through which the country was to be regenerated.

Document 36
"THE MARSHAL PROTECTS THE FAMILY"

Document

Source: The Welch Collection.

Analysis

Document 36 is the front cover of *Vichy* magazine published in 1942. The magazine was typical of the propaganda literature produced that emphasized marriage, family values, maternity facilities provided by the state, and the financial and ideological inducements to all families to have at least four children. Marshal Pétain is depicted as the encouraging, avuncular father-figure of the nation, constantly surrounded by adoring, young children. The slogan of the *Révolution nationale*, "Travail, Famille, Patrie," and the propaganda media that propounded these imperatives gave prominence to the importance of large families and stressed each family member's vital role in France's future. Inside, the magazine quotes a speech that Marshal Pétain made in 1940 to the youth of France in which he repudiates the motto of the French Republic. *Liberté, Égalité, Fraternité*: "When our young people . . . approach adult life, we shall say to them that real liberty cannot be exercised except under the shelter of a guiding authority, which they must respect, which they must obey. . . . We shall then tell them that equality [should] set itself within the framework of a hierarchy, founded on the diversity of office and merits. . . . Finally, we shall tell them that there is no way of having true brotherhood except within those natural groups, the family, the town, and the homeland.[1]

In it we see all these factors featured in one very simple design. Stylistically, it is similar to the *völkisch* posters and paintings that were such a dominant feature of Nazi art and propaganda. Vichy sought an essentially anti-modern counter-revolution. The Right in France, with strength in the aristocracy and among Catholics, had never accepted the republican traditions of the French Revolution. It demanded a return to traditional lines of culture and religion and embraced authoritarianism, while dismissing democracy. The message of the "New Order," which spread throughout Europe following Nazi occupation looked to the past for inspiration in order to provide meaning for the present and hope for the future. It called for a regeneration of Europe along racial principles espoused by National Socialism and cobbled together with a vague medieval folklore that would allow industrial mass society to be controlled and shaped by a modern, centralized, authoritarian state.

The idealized agrarian and artisan lifestyle that was closely associated with the "New Order," dominate the bottom of the poster; the agricultural worker and the blacksmith work contentedly, while the mother-figure in peasant dress looks lovingly at her four children. The French capital, symbolized by the Eiffel Tower and modern industry (smoking towers) are relegated to the background, revealing an ordinary church spire is larger than the national symbol of the Eiffel Tower. The focus of the poster is very much on a benevolent Pétain as national standard bearer, draped in the tricolor and wearing a military uniform. The Vichy regime, which dropped the word "republic" in favor of "the French state," maintained the use of the tricolor, but Pétain used as his personal standard a version of the flag with, in the white stripe, an axe made with a seven star-studded marshal's baton that can be seen in the poster holding up the edifice of the new French state and its slogan, "Work, Family, Fatherland" This axe is called the "Francisque" in reference to the ancient Frankish throwing axe and together with the double-headed hatchet arranged so as to resemble the fasces, symbol of the Italian fascists.[2] Both the motto and the Vichy axe appeared on reverse sides of the two franc coin in 1943.

Marshal Pétain blamed the Third Republic's democracy for France's humiliating military defeat. The immediate requirement was Franco-German reconciliation. Spurred on by Pierre Laval, the regime's principal architect and by the Philippe Henriot, head of Vichy propaganda, the regime was vehemently anti-British and, after a meeting with Hitler, Pétain publicly called for collaboration with the Germans. Having condemned the armistice and Pétain's collaborationist stance, Vichy propaganda presented the British as war criminals and the Germans as saviors of Europe from Bolshevism. In October 1940, Jews were excluded from the administration, the armed forces, entertainment, arts, media, and certain professions, such as teaching, law, and medicine.

Document 37 is a photograph of the major anti-Jewish exhibition held in September 1941 in the Palais Berlitz, Paris. A Vichy newsreel covering the event claimed that thousands of Frenchmen had visited the exhibition in the first few days since it opened. Titled "The Jew and France," the exhibition aimed to "show the Jewish peril in all aspects of French life." It also blamed the Jews for France's humiliating defeat in 1940. The exhibition was vehemently anti-Semitic and produced artifacts that claimed to show that Jews were racially inferior and described their physical appearance in grotesquely disparaging terms.[3] The large poster of the exhibition that can be seen in the photograph shows a stereotypical Eastern ghetto Jew with claw-like hands clasping the globe.

Document 37

"THE JEW AND FRANCE": A PHOTOGRAPH OF THE MAJOR ANTI-JEWISH EXHIBITION HELD IN PARIS IN 1941

Document

Source: Bundesarchiv Bild 146-1975-041-07.

Analysis

While Pétain became the figurehead for the regime, Philippe Henriot largely shaped its propaganda becoming the government's spokesman with the nickname of the "French Goebbels." In 1943, he was appointed secretary of state for information[4] and together with fellow collaborationists, Jaques Doriot and Jean Hérold-Paquis, regularly broadcast on the Vichy mouthpiece, *Radio Paris*. Together they developed a war of propaganda against the Free French Forces and the BBC. Vichy propaganda was vehemently anti-British; and from 1942, Jean Hérold-Paquis broadcast daily news reports on Radio Paris, in which he regularly called for the "destruction" of Britain. His catchphrase was "England, like Carthage, shall be destroyed!" Its broadcasts were pitched directly against the BBC broadcasts of *Radio Londres* (each news bulletin to the French people under occupation began with the famous "Ici Londres") by Free French figures like Pierre Dac, who sang the taunting refrain, *Radio Paris ment, Radio Paris ment, Radio Paris est allemand* ("Radio Paris lies, Radio Paris lies, Radio Paris is German"), to the tune of *La Cucaracha*.

Document 38

"WITH THAT 'DE GAULLE,' YOU WON'T CATCH ANYTHING, LADIES AND GENTLEMEN . . ." (CIRCA 1941)

Document

Source: Musee de l'Armee Invalides, France (Dist. RMN-Grand Palais).

Analysis

Document 38 is a Vichy anti-British poster. The poster suggests that the Free French are agents of the British and the Jews. Charles de Gaulle, the leader of the Free French, is depicted as a fish-hook—or float—who is dangled in front of the French sailor by Winston Churchill and a cowering Jewish banker clutching a bag with the pound sterling sign. They are both "fishing" from a patched up little boat, *Rule Britannia*. The reference to Dakar is "Operation Menace," the incident in September 1940 when the British and the Free French attempted unsuccessfully to capture the strategic port in French West Africa that remained loyal to the Vichy government. The battleship in the foreground of the poster ("Richelieu") was one of the most advanced warships in the French fleet and it was in the forefront (even though it was only 95 percent complete) in withstanding the attempt to sink the French Fleet.

Document 39

THE FRENCH EMPIRE GAME (1942)

Document

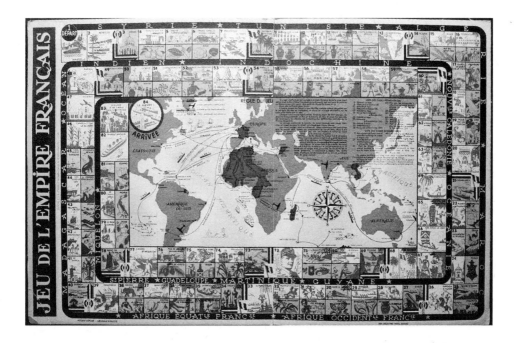

Source: The Welch Collection.

Analysis

Children were both the subject and the target of much of the propaganda produced during this period. Among the panoply of propaganda aimed at French youth are the so-called goose games (*Jeu d'oie*—similar to snakes and ladders). The game with the Vichy axe emblem was aimed primarily at French youth but was also distributed among other places to French POW camps in Germany. It represents a perfect example of Vichy propaganda that aimed to inspire a new form of French nationalism. The squares with a goose are replaced by squares with the axe symbol and squares bearing key words of the "New Order" allow the player to move forward. Such words are "solidarity," "spirit of justice," "youth movements," "return to the land," "military service," and "marriage with four children" (the big family has pride of place on the final square). Laziness, discouragement, selfishness, black market—all these squares mean the player has to go back, whilst landing on Marshall Petain allows the player to complete the game in one go. Many "goose games" from the Petain era such as Document 39 ("the French Empire Game") boast of the marvels of the empire, which require 2 circuits and 84 squares. You need all that to travel round such a huge colonial empire—the final pride of an occupied France. Starting in Marseille and ending in Le Havre, France's colonial products, the charms of tourism and work of the Pasteur Institute in the field of health are all showcased. The huge map of the empire has pride of place at the center of the game and carefully lists all the French colonies, but there is no mention of the French occupation by the Germans. The board game was intended to inspire French youth and inculcate the conservative values that would secure the "New Order" in Vichy France. These values would continue to be disseminated by Vichy propaganda for a further two years. Following the Allied invasion of France in June 1944 (see Documents 41, 42) and the subsequent Liberation of France in the summer of 1944, the Free French Provisional Government under the leadership of General Charles de Gaulle succeeded Vichy as France's government. The bitter divisions in the 1930s and the impact of collaboration in World War II continue to resound through modern French politics.[5]

Notes

1. Maréchal Pétain, *Politique sociale de l'avenir* (Future Social Policy), *La Revue des Deux Mondes*, September 15, 1940.

2. During this same period, the Free French used a tricolor with, in the white stripe, a red Cross of Lorraine.

3. The newsreel, *Les Actualités Mondiales* (September 12, 1941) can be downloaded: video/AFE86001433/inauguration-de-l-exposition-le-juif-et-la-france-au-p alais-berlitz.fr.html. One exhibit refers to a "typical" Jewish face as "fleshy, open mouth, thick lips, wide, massive and protruding ears, heavily hooked nose . . . flabby features."

4. On January 6, 1944, Henriot was appointed as the French minister of information and on June 28, 1944, he was assassinated by the Maquis. For a wider discussion of Vichy France see, J. Jackson, *France: The Dark Years, 1940–1944* (Oxford University Press, Oxford, 2003) and R. O. Paxton, *Vichy France: Old Guard and New Order 1940–1944* (Columbia University Press, New York, 2001). For an analysis of Vichy propaganda see, L. Gervereau and D. Peschanski (eds.), *La Propagande Sous Vichy, 1940–1944* (BDIC, Paris, 1990).

5. In 2014, the debate was reopened with the publication of a controversial bestseller, which claims that France's collaborationist wartime regime has been misunderstood and that it tried to save French Jews from Nazi death camps. See, Eric Zemmour, *Le Suicide français. Les 40 années qui ont défait La France* (Paris: Albin Michel, 2014).

Chapter 20

"Black" Propaganda and Operation OVERLORD (D-Day)

In the popular view, propaganda is commonly associated with the idea of the "big lie," but in fact, it operates on many different levels. It may be "black," but it may also be "grey" or "white." And when it comes to conflict, actual warfare may be bolstered by "psychological warfare." Broadly speaking, these three terms can be defines as follows:

White: truthful and not strongly biased, where the source of information is acknowledged.

Grey: largely truthful, containing no information that can be proven wrong; the source is not identified.

Black: inherently deceitful, information given in the product is attributed to a source that was not responsible for its creation.[1]

Sometimes there is complete openness about the source of a piece of propaganda. However, on other occasions, it is necessary to conceal the source's identity in order to achieve certain objectives. "Black" propaganda (sometimes referred to as "covert" propaganda) tries to conceal its own identity by purporting to emanate from someone or somewhere other than the true source. It is, therefore, often quite difficult to detect black propaganda until after all the facts are known.

During the early phase of World War II, the Nazis operated at least three radio stations that sought to give the impression that they were broadcasting somewhere in Britain. One was called Radio Free Caledonia and claimed to be the voice of Scottish nationalism; another referred to itself as the Workers' Challenge Station and disseminated unorthodox left-wing views; a third, the New British Broadcasting Station, provided news bulletins and comments in the style of the BBC but with a concealed pro-German bias. None of these stations reached large audiences, and they only broadcast for a few hours a day. The aim of this black propaganda was to undermine the morale of the British people, particularly during the Battle of Britain in 1940.

White broadcasts by the British Broadcasting Company (BBC) to Europe proved extremely popular, as was demonstrated by the famous "V for Victory" campaign. It was unwittingly launched in January 1941 following an unplanned reference in a BBC Belgian program. Before long, resistance fighters were daubing the "V" sign on buildings throughout Belgium, Holland, and France. The Germans attempted to claim "V" for themselves and began broadcasting as their station identification the opening bars of Beethoven's Fifth Symphony, which matched the Morse code for the letter "V." But the British government was concerned that the campaign was encouraging premature hopes for victory and ordered an end to it in May 1942. Even so, the campaign had demonstrated the influence of radio and the role it could play in encouraging resistance amongst the occupied peoples of Europe, dominated by Nazi news broadcasts.[2]

Later in the war, the British (who sometimes conflated black propaganda with "political warfare," i.e., psychological warfare) set up their own "black" radio station, which claimed to be an official German station run by German soldiers for those on the Western Front. At the same time, leaflets in the form of newspapers were dropped over the German lines purporting to originate from (nonexistent) German resistance organizations. Fake ration cards and other ingenious devices were also employed.

Black propaganda, by definition, seeks to deceive and encompasses all types of deception, meaning not only leaflets, posters, and radio stations but also including postage stamps, television stations, and now even the Internet. This type of propaganda consequently receives the most attention when it is revealed. The success or failure of it largely depends on the receiver's willingness to accept the authenticity of the source and the content of the message. For black propaganda to achieve its aims, great care has to be taken to place the message within the social, political, and cultural experiences of the target audience and to take similar care with the manner in which it is disseminated

During World War II, the British government continued to use the term "political warfare"—based on its Political Warfare Executive—until the Americans joined in after 1941, when the preferred US term "psychological warfare" replaced it. The Political Warfare Executive (PWE) was a British clandestine body created in 1941 to produce and disseminate both white and black propaganda, with the aim of damaging enemy morale and sustaining the morale of the occupied countries. PWE's brief was simple: "to deliver a decisive blow at the heart of the enemy's morale by any means necessary," which included both the use of white and black propaganda—largely by means of leaflets and radio broadcasts—in an effort to weaken the German will to fight.

Allied Psychological Warfare branches were established in the various theaters of action, the largest of which was set up in North Africa in November 1942. As part of the preparations for the invasion of Europe, the Psychological Warfare Division was established at Supreme Headquarters Allied Expeditionary Forces (PWD/SHAEF). Although this suggested greater inter-Allied cooperation than was, in fact, the case, the British and Americans were united in their overall approach to psychological warfare, which was based on a distinction between white and black propaganda. PWE and SHAEF proved particularly effective in supporting the campaign for the liberation of Europe (Operation OVERLORD or D-Day).

A group of fictitious radio stations ostensibly broadcast conversations between underground cells of disaffected German soldiers. They were, in fact, broadcast by a secret transmitter in Britain, codenamed "Aspidistra," and this constituted the principal black propaganda technique employed by the Allies, reinforced by secret agents disseminating false rumors. Since it was purportedly coming from within occupied Europe, the black propaganda did not have to worry about lies or false promises. As a result, the rumors disseminated became, at times, quite fantastic. One of the most ridiculous was that the British had imported 200 man-eating sharks from Australia, which had been released in the English Channel to eat Germans whose invasion boats had been sunk!

The arrival of *Daily Express* journalist Sefton Delmer had brought about a drastic change in the status and dissemination of PWE's "black" section—most notably the black radio stations (See Document 3). Under Delmer's leadership, PWE created a number of clandestine radio stations including *Gustav Siegfried Eins*, *Soldatensender Calais*, and *Kurzwellesender Atlantik*. They claimed to be illegal radio stations operating within Nazi Germany. The programs for *Gustav Siegfried Eins* were recorded on glass disc and then taken to the short wave radio stations in Britain. They featured "Der Chef," an unrepentant Nazi, who disparaged both Churchill ("that flatfooted bastard of a drunken Jew") and the "Party Communists" who betrayed the Nazi revolution. Few Germans listening to this could conceive that British propagandists would dare to refer to their country's leader in such disparaging terms. *Soldatensender Calais* operated from 6 p.m. local time to dawn. Programs were live from the purposely built broadcast studio in Bedfordshire and presented by Agnes Bernelle using the codename "Vicky." *Soldatensender Calais* broadcast a combination of good music, "cover" support of the war, and "dirt,"—items inserted to demoralize German forces. Delmer's propaganda stories included spreading rumors that foreign workers were sleeping with the wives of German soldiers serving overseas.[3] Stories also linked to a daily "grey" German-language newspaper titled *Nachrichten für die Truppe*.

Many areas of Western Europe were targeted with propaganda prior to D-Day, in order to give the Germans no indication as to where and when the invasion would come. PWE also supported the deception operations put in place to protect Overlord, indicating to the Germans even after D-Day that the main landing was still to come. Inflatable Sherman tanks were used during Operation FORTITUDE, one of the three major deception operations making up Operation BODYGUARD.[4]

To deceive the German observation planes, which their anti-aircraft defenses did their best to avoid, the local estuaries, creeks, and harbors were crammed with dummy landing craft. A large numbers of inflatable rubber tanks were positioned in the fields. Plywood vehicles and guns lined the roadsides. At night, convoys of lorries—always the same ones—drove back and forth across the region. For the benefit of the Germans, a team of technicians maintained constant radio traffic between totally fictitious units. Operation FORTITUDE proved highly successful. Long after June 6, Hitler remained convinced that the Normandy landings were a diversionary tactic to induce him to move his troops away from the Pas-de-Calais, so that a decisive attack could then be launched there. He therefore kept his best units in readiness there, until the end of July, desperately scanning an empty horizon, while the fate of the war was being decided in Normandy.

Prior to D-day, PWE was becoming increasingly integrated with Office of War Information (OWI), and due to the importance of the operation, SHAEF (Supreme Headquarters Allied Expeditionary Force) saw it as necessary that the two organizations draw up a single political warfare plan for France. As a result, PWE and OWI came up with a plan that covered two main requirements—both in terms of men and material that would be required for (1) "the conduct of propaganda and publicity inside the released area and (2) the use of the "released area" as a base for the conduct of political warfare, along with aims and objectives of the campaign. The two organizations were integrated by SHAEF as it was acknowledged that while "OWI could supply the men and the machines necessary for propaganda in the field and in the liberated areas; PWE could supply the political experience and political doctrine necessary."

Notwithstanding their support of resistance groups throughout Europe but particularly France, PWE also targeted German troops deployed in Western Europe in order to damage the morale of both the ordinary soldier and their commanders. Such propaganda was intended to undermine the will of German soldiers to continue to fight in the West by making the troops feel abandoned by their leaders—and so affect their effectiveness on the battlefield. Well known are the malingering instructions delivered to the enemy forces and workers in Germany.

Document 40

A "BLACK" PROPAGANDA BOOKLET *KRANKHEIT RETTET* ("ILLNESS SAVES") (1944)

Document

I. KAPITEL.

Hilfe für Alle.

In diesem Kapitel findest du Krankheiten beschrieben, die für alle Arbeiter und Arbeiterinnen, gleichgültig in welcher Art von Betrieb sie arbeiten, geeignet sind. Wer immer genug hat von der totalen Antreiberei und sich für eine Zeit oder für dauernd ins Privatleben zurückziehen möchte, wer sich die Reste seiner Gesundheit für bessere Zeiten nach dem Kriege aufheben will, der findet hier, was er braucht.

1. Schwere Rückenschmerzen.

Es kommt sehr häufig vor, daß sich Leute mit Rückenschmerzen krank melden. Sie behaupten, daß sie sich nicht bücken können, und beklagen sich besonders über Schmerzen beim Wiederaufrichten. Der Arzt wird meistens, und oft mit Recht, solche Beschwerden als „Muskelkater" abtun und dem Mann nur raten, die Schmerzen „wegzuarbeiten". Wenn du den Arzt davon überzeugen willst, daß in deinem Fall eine ernsthaftere Beschwerde vorliegt, die dich wirklich arbeitsunfähig macht, mußt du dir schon ein bißchen Mühe geben und dir die richtigen Symptome sorgfältig einüben. Das wird folgendermaßen gemacht:

Rechts und links vom Rückgrat, etwa in der Höhe des Gürtels, findest du je einen dicken Muskel, der das ganze Rückgrat entlang läuft. (Abbildung 2.) Du nimmst einen kleinen, runden Gegenstand etwa eine kleine Wall- oder große Haselnuß, und steckst

20

sie unter den Hosenbund so, daß sie vom Gürtel festgehalten wird und genau auf die äußere Kante eines dieser Muskeln drückt.

Du wirst spüren, wie die Nuß bei jedem Schritt und bei jeder Bewegung, wie Bücken, Wiederaufrichten usw., auf den Muskel drückt. Du versuchst nun, dich so zu bewegen, daß die Nuß nicht auf den Muskel drückt.

Abbildung 2.

Zeigt den starken Muskel (latissimus dorsi), der sich rechts und links des Rückgrats befindet. Der Kreis am Ende der gestrichelten Linie zeigt an, wo die Nuß getragen werden muß. Der Gürtel ist angedeutet, um die richtige Höhe anzugeben.

Angenommen, du hast die Nuß auf dem linken der beiden Muskeln. Dann wirst du sie erst einmal fühlen, wenn du beim Schritt das linke Bein nach vorn bringst. Versuche nun, vorsichtig und langsam zu gehen und so, daß du beim Vorbringen des linken Beines keinen Druck spürst. Das heißt: Du mußt lernen, dich zu bewegen, ohne diesen Muskel zu benutzen. Das ist der einzige Zweck dieser Übung. Wie das gemacht wird, mußt du selber herausfinden, es ist nicht so schwer,

21

Source: The Welch Collection.

Analysis

Document 40 is a very small, pocket-size, booklet *Krankheit rettet* ("Illness saves"). Instructions were given to the German soldiers on how to fake illnesses in such a way that they would be sent back home or at least secure extra *Fronturlaub* (leave from the front). On the two pages shown here, instructions are given on how to simulate serious pains in the back.

German civilians were also viewed as legitimate targets of PWE propaganda. Once the Americans had entered the war, PWE was able to acquire a powerful medium wave transmitter code-named Aspidistra, which enabled

PWE to reach the more popular medium wave sets of the bulk of the German civilian population—in spite of draconian penalties imposed by the Nazis for those caught listening. Aspidistra broadcasts attempted to undermine loyalty to the Nazi regime by slowing down civilian contributions to the war effort. The overriding aim of PWE's black propaganda was to drive a wedge between the German people and the Nazi leadership—or as PWE put it: "exploiting and canalizing the political ferments behind enemy lines." To this end, PWE used leaflets and postcards on a vast scale and by March 1944, 265 million leaflets had been manufactured and dropped. PWE's black propaganda teased out the idea of a split in privileges between people and the party—the message being that Nazi "high-ups" secured privileges for themselves at the expense of Germany's war economy and the ordinary people.

Document 41

D-DAY EDITION OF *NACHRICHTEN FÜR DIE TRUPPE* (NEWS FOR THE TROOPS), AIR-DROPPED NEWSPAPER AIMED AT GERMAN TROOPS (1944)

Document

Source: National Archives, Kew, FO 898/456 "D" Leaflet operations and reports.

Analysis

In addition to strategic and tactical leaflets and postcards, a great many news-papers and miniature magazines were produced for dropping from the air during World War II. These fell into two categories, those such as *Le Courrier de l'Air*, the French language newspaper which was intended to boost morale and give information to the inhabitants of the occupied countries and others like *Nachrichten für die Truppe* (News for the Troops), the world's first airborne daily newspaper which intended to lower the morale of enemy troops. Printed in German, the first edition of *Nachrichten für die Truppe* came out on April 25, 1944, with a print run of 200,000, but by D-Day this had risen to a million and continued daily at this level until the German surrender on May 8, 1945. This four-page paper contained timely and accurate military information and news from the German home front designed to gain the German soldier's confidence in the truthfulness of the source and to keep him fully informed of the defeats suffered by the Germans and their allies. On occasion some "grey" or "black" items were included, especially in the days leading up to the Normandy invasion.

An "imminent danger" leaflet for the French population in the operational zone was dropped on D-Day, an hour before the intensive bombing began. Two days after the landing, 1.5 million Safe Conduct Leaflets (*Passierscheine*), signed by Supreme Commander Dwight Eisenhower, were then dropped by Bomber Command intended to create "an atmosphere in which the German soldier feel able to surrender." Interrogation of German POWs proved their effectiveness, and these Safe Conduct Pass leaflets carried a high barter value in the German lines. For the immediate period, 32 million leaflets were prepared translated into German, French, Dutch, Danish, and Norwegian. Translation of the Eisenhower D-Day statement into all languages had foremost priority.

Once the Nazis had realized that D-day had actually been launched, they rather ponderously produced their own counter-propaganda, eventually dropping large numbers of leaflets at the American and British troops that had landed on the Normandy beaches and distributed further leaflets with a different propaganda message over southern England.

Document 42

NAZI LEAFLETS FOR AMERICAN AND BRITISH (ENGLISH) SOLDIERS, 10 DAYS AFTER D-DAY (1944)

Document

CAUGHT LIKE FOXES IN A TRAP

English and American soldiers !

Why has Jerry waited ten days after the landings to use his so called secret weapon behind your back ? Doesn't that strike you as queer ?

It looks very much as though after waiting for you to cross the Channel, **he had set a TRAP for you.**

You're fighting at present on a very narrow strip of coast, the extent of which has been so far regulated by the Germans.

You are using up an enormous number of men and huge quantities of material.

Meanwhile the Robot-planes, flying low, scatter over London and Southern England explosives, the power and incendiary eff ency of which are without precedent. **They spread death and destruction in the towns and harbours,** which should be sending you much needed supplies.

They are cutting the bridge to your bases

In addition to the destruction and panic at home, trafic is disorganised, ships, even hospital ships, are held up.

How long can you keep up this foolish « invasion » in those circumstances ?

It's up to you to think of the best way to get out of the TRAP in wich you are CAUGHT.

Time is precious. To-morrow may be too late.

Source: The Welch Collection.

Analysis

Document 42 is a leaflet that attempts to sow seeds of doubt in the minds of Allied troops. Note that it is printed 10 days after the first Normandy landings. The leaflet maintains that the Nazis had *not* been caught unawares by Operation OVERLORD (which, of course, they had), but rather had lured the troops into a trap ("Caught like Foxes in a Trap"). Meanwhile, it claims London and southern England are suffering "death and destruction" by "Robot planes" and asks "how long can you keep up this foolish 'invasion'"?—implying that the best way of getting out of this "trap" is to surrender (note the typographical error in the leaflet).

Document 43

V-1. THIS LEAFLET HAS A LONG PROPAGANDA MESSAGE ON THE BACK ENTITLED "NEWS FROM THE CENSORED BRITISH PRESS" (1944)

Document

Source: Galerie Bilderwelt/Getty Images.

Analysis

Document 43 is a leaflet dropped over Britain that takes up the theme of the "Robot planes." The V-1 referred to on this leaflet is a reference to the V-1 flying bomb (nicknamed the "doodlebug").[5] Southern Britain is in flames (so it claims), as a result of the destruction it had wreaked. The other side of the leaflet consists of numerous examples of alleged British censorship that prevented the media from revealing the "true" military situation. Graphically, the leaflets are effectively simple. Goebbels had been trumpeting the V-1 and the V-2 rockets as "revenge" weapons (the V for *Vergeltung*) claiming on a special radio broadcast "The Question of Retaliation" that Britain could no longer defend itself against these pilotless guided missiles. These so-called miracle weapons were eventually deployed in mid-June 1944 but failed to live up to Nazi expectations, although they did cause havoc and terror in London for a relatively short period.[6]

Documents 42 and 43 illustrate the Nazi propaganda machine's desperate response to Operation OVERLORD. However, at this stage of the war, no amount of propaganda could undermine confidence in an Allied victory. Newspaper reports, radio broadcasts, and film newsreels all confirmed that D-Day had been a military success and that Paris would soon be liberated. Nazi armed forces and propaganda were everywhere in retreat. PWE and SHAEF's contribution in the propaganda war that led up to Operation OVERLORD should not be underestimated. It created and disseminated a multifaceted propaganda campaign that skillfully incorporated "black" and sometime "grey" propaganda. In the words of a PWE official, "The fighting services attack the body, we attack the mind."

Notes

1. For a detailed "historical" analysis of changing perceptions and definition of propaganda including different "shades" see, N. Cull, D. Culbert, and D. Welch, *Propaganda and Mass Persuasion. A Historical Encyclopedia, 1500 to the Present* (Santa Barbara, CA: ABC-CLIO, 2004), 41–43, 151–155, 317–323, 425–426.

2. Cf. P. Taylor, *Munitions of the Mind. A History of Propaganda from the Ancient World to the Present Day* (Manchester: Manchester University Press, 1995), 223–224.

3. Of these broadcasts Joseph Goebbels wrote in his diary: "The so-called *Soldatensender* which evidently originates in England and sometimes uses the same wavelength as our *Deutschlandsender* is certainly giving us something to thinks about. It does a clever job of propaganda, and from what is put out on the air, one gathers that the English know exactly what they have destroyed in our cities." Quoted in A. Rhodes, *Propaganda. The Art of Persuasion: World War II* (Leicester: Magna Books, 1993), 114.

4. For a wider discussion of the deception operations leading up to D-Day see, M. Barbier, *D-Day Deception: Operation Fortitude and the Normandy Invasion* (Mechanicsburg, PA: Stackpole Books, 2009).

5. The first V-1 was launched at London on June 3, 1944. At its peak, more than 100 V-1s a day were fired at southeast England, 9,521 in total, decreasing in number as sites were overrun until October 1944, when the last V-1 site in range of Britain was captured overrun by Allied forces.

6. For a more detailed discussion of the Nazi propaganda of "retaliation" (*Vergeltung*) see, Welch, *The Third Reich*, 144–156.

Chapter 21

Images of the Enemy

Perhaps the most identifiable stylistic device in propaganda is the use of contrasts. Not only do strong contrasts contain a greater emotional intensity than more subtle nuances, but they also guide the audience's sympathies with more certainty. Propaganda based on contrasts is full of confrontations between good and evil, beauty and "the beast," order and chaos; in each case, the contrast serves to force the individual into a desired, established commitment to a particular view. In this ultimate purpose, propaganda is aided by our psychological need for value judgments in simple black-and-white terms. This is particularly so if a country is in a state of crisis or war, when there is an increasing need for a simplification of the issues. At such times, the "other side" becomes totally malevolent and everyone gathers around the symbols of unity.

Political propaganda therefore thrives in times of uncertainty, and fueling hatred is generally its most fruitful aid. In any society, people cannot be kept too long at a pitch of sacrifice and conviction in aid of a cause. Even in regimes that have demanded a relentless fanaticism, such as the Third Reich or during periods in the Soviet Union, some form of diversion was needed. Hatred of an enemy can be manipulated to fulfil such a need. The very immediate, spontaneous nature of hatred, a simple and sometimes violent emotion, can be aroused through the most elementary of means. In essence, it consists in attributing one's own misfortunes to an outsider. Frustrated people need to hate, because hatred—when shared with others—is the most potent of all unifying emotions; or, as Heinrich Heine put it in the 19th century, "What Christian love cannot achieve is affected by a common hatred." Whether the object of hatred is the Bolshevik, the Jew, the Muslim or the Anglo-Saxon, such propaganda has its best chance of success when it clearly designates a target as the source of all misery or suffering, providing the target it chooses is not too powerful. The aim of propaganda is to identify the object of this hatred in order to solidify the feelings of hatred.

Clearly, identifying an object to hate means exploiting stereotypes—conventional figures that come to be regarded as representative of particular classes, races, nations, and so on. Indeed, this is one of the most striking means by which different propaganda media such as the cinema and television have influenced social attitudes, changing or reinforcing opinions. The American social scientist Walter Lippmann developed the term "stereotype" to describe the knowledge people thought they possessed—that is, knowledge based on myths or dreams. He believed in the power of the myth, or stereotype, to arouse popular—enthusiasm, and he argued that abstract ideas and concepts such as national pride were more real to the masses than actual realities. In this context, propaganda gives individuals the stereotypes they no longer take the trouble to work out for themselves; it furnishes stereotypes in the form of slogans or labels. The recognition of stereotypes is therefore an important part of understanding the use of anti-symbols and the portrayal of the enemy in propaganda. Not only does it provide a target that can be attacked, but it also offers a scapegoat, the easiest means of diverting public attentions from genuine social and political problems at home. Stereotypes invariably come ready-made, having evolved, whether consciously or subconsciously, over a considerable period of time. They frequently attach themselves to myths associated with other nations, races, or groups. In propaganda terminology, there are two kinds of images of the enemy that emerge: the enemy from "within," and the enemy from "without." Propaganda is usually concerned with the latter—particularly in times of war—but not exclusively, as the following two case studies will show.

Nazi Anti-Semitic Propaganda

Anti-Jewish and anti-Bolshevik motifs were central to the Nazi *Weltanschauung* ("world view"). The Nazi movement had developed and finally emerged from a struggle in which communists together with the Jews formed the main target of Nazi violence and invective. Indeed, by claiming a Marxist-inspired Jewish-Bolshevik conspiracy, Nazi propaganda was able, at times, to fuse these two enemies into one. However, for a brief period following the defeat of France in 1940, German propagandists switched to targeting the British. Once Britain had declared war on Germany in September 1939, it became a distinctive enemy and object of hatred in Nazi propaganda. Throughout the early part of the summer of 1940, as the struggle for control of the skies above Britain took place, anti-British propaganda reached a new crescendo, claiming that it was only a matter of time before Britain's fate was sealed. Propaganda emphasized British hypocrisy and "plutocracy." Churchill in particular was targeted and mercilessly lampooned. One famous poster depicted him as an American-style gangster ("The Sniper"), brandishing a machine gun (See Document 11). The SD Reports (of the *Sicherheitsdienst* secret police) suggested that German hatred of Britain, incited by incessant propaganda, was now widespread.

It is surprising, though, to discover that the Nazis used humor—albeit rarely—to undermine their enemies. In 1941, they released the anti-British documentary film *Soldaten von Morgen* ("Soldiers of Tomorrow"). It was a film made by the Hitler Youth for the Hitler Youth, but it was also shown widely in the Third Reich.[1] The film takes the form of a Hitler Youth theatrical skit on the English public-school system and the resultant effete degeneracy supposed to result from such an education. Leading British political figures such as Churchill, and both the former and current foreign secretaries Lord Halifax and Anthony Eden, are cited as examples. British youth is ridiculed quite savagely. The film ends with disheveled British troops being captured at Dunkirk. The morale of the story is clear: effete young English schoolboys turn into easily captured British troops. The second half of the film offers an unfavorable comparison with the virile qualities and athletic activities of German youth, who are seen fencing, gliding, parachute jumping, horse-riding, and participating in "mock" battles along with a final parade.

Soldaten von Morgen reflects the euphoric nature of Nazi propaganda in general during this period. Goebbels referred to the British as the "Jews among the Aryans"—a decaying society dominated by Jews. Despite the propaganda, the Battle of Britain turned out to be a failure not only for the Luftwaffe but also for Nazi propaganda, which was not prepared to admit a British defensive victory in the air. Goebbels's anti-British propaganda suffered a further setback in May 1941, when the leading Nazi Rudolf Hess flew to Scotland in a desperate attempt to bring the British to their senses—only to end up in ignominious captivity.

While the British represented a clear enemy without—one whom the Germans were actually fighting in a conventional war—Nazi ideology had simultaneously identified Jews as the enemy within. Anti-Semitism was not only the core of Nazi ideology, but the Jewish stereotype that developed from it provided the focal point for the feelings of aggression inherent in the ideology. Before 1939, anti-Semitism was propagated chiefly through the German educational system and the press. Three major campaigns were waged: the boycott of Jewish shops in 1933, the anti-Semitic Nuremberg Laws in 1935, and the destruction of Jewish-owned property in the *Reichskristallnacht* of 1938.

An important function of Nazi propaganda was therefore to disseminate Nazi racial ideology. Press directives had ensured that racial issues would figure prominently in the daily newspapers. Goebbels had even suggested that not one week should pass without a discussion of racial-political questions. Emphasis would often be placed on aspects of Jewish "criminality" against German interests. Before the proclamation of the Nuremberg Laws, for example, a "public enlightenment" program had been instigated to demonstrate the history of Jewish "crimes" and "conspiracies." A similar campaign followed the *Kristallnacht*, when synagogues were torched and vandalized. Nothing illustrates the campaign more clearly than the Nazi use of film. In coordination with propaganda campaigns in other media, a number of films were prepared, in an attempt to make the German people aware of the "dangers" posed by Jewry and also to rationalize any measures that were, or might be, taken by the regime, either publicly or in secret.

Document 44

POSTER FROM THE FILM *DER EWIGE JUDE* (1940): A VEHEMENTLY ANTI-SEMITIC DIATRIBE THAT CLAIMED TO BE "A DOCUMENTARY ABOUT WORLD JUDAISM"

Document

Source: Imperial War Museum (Art.IWM PST 8327), © IWM.

Analysis

The outbreak of World War II allowed the Nazi regime to radicalize incrementally its anti-Jewish campaign. The war hastened the process of "cumulative radicalization," which started with intimidation and persecution and culminated in a network of extermination camps (all outside Germany) in occupied Poland and the slaughter of 6 million Jews. As we have seen in 1940, three major anti-Semitic films were released—*Die Rothschilds* ("The Rothschilds"), *Jud Süss* ("Jew Süss"), and *Der ewige Jude* ("The Eternal—or Wandering—Jew") to justify the "Final Solution" to the "Jewish problem." (Cf. Document 44). The most notorious and virulent of all anti-Semitic films is *Der ewige Jude*, which ran the gamut of Nazi allegations against Jews and was intended to prepare the German people for the genocide of the Final Solution. The film begins with scenes from the Warsaw ghetto, designed to show the reluctance of Jews to undertake creative labor, and it continues by depicting the migration of Jews and their attempts to assimilate with European peoples. Animated maps show how the Jews, starting from Palestine ("the spiritual center for international Jewry"), diffused across the world; furthermore, the 19th century "with its vague ideas of human equality and freedom, gave the Jew a powerful impetus," according to the film's narration. This diffusion is illustrated as a dense network over the map, resembling festering sores. The film then cuts to a sequence of rats devouring grain and scurrying in packs, filling the screen, in an analogy between rats and Jews that Hitler had first used in *Mein Kampf*. The commentary continues:

> Comparable with the Jewish wanderings through history are the mass migrations of an equally restless animal, the rat. . . . Wherever rats appear they bring ruin, they ravage human property and foodstuffs. In this way they spread disease: plague, leprosy, typhoid, cholera; dysentery, etc. They are cunning, cowardly, and cruel and are found mostly in packs. In the animal world they represent the element of craftiness and subterranean destruction—no different from the Jews among mankind!

By contrasting Jewish individualism and "self-seeking" with the National Socialist ideal of a "people's community" (*Volksgemeinschaft*), and by claiming that Jews were only motivated by money, it was possible to demonstrate that Judaism was the total antithesis of the cherished values of the German cultural tradition as interpreted by Nazi ideology. But more important, the constant analogy made with rats and parasites suggested that the Jew differed from the Aryan not only in body but, more significantly, in soul, for the Jew had no soul. The implication was that here was a menace that had to be "resisted." Thus, the conclusion to be drawn from watching such films was that the killing of Jews was not a crime but a necessity: Jews, after all, were not human beings but pests, which had to be exterminated. *Der ewige Jude* represents a form of National Socialist "realism" depicting not so much what was, but what ought to have been, in accordance with the preconceived notion of Nazi racial ideology. Having previewed the film before its release, Goebbels recorded in his diary the "scenes so horrific and brutal in their explicitness that one's blood runs cold. One shudders at such barbarism. This Jewry must be eliminated."

Despite such attempts at whipping up anti-Semitism, the regime encountered problems. At precisely the time that Jewish persecution was being intensified and the details of the Final Solution were falling into place, during the summer and autumn of 1941, the SD Reports were noting either boredom with, or massive indifference to, the "Jewish Question" among the population (Cf. Document 31). Ironically, such indifference proved fatal for the Jews. Interest in the fate of Jews had, in fact, rapidly evaporated after the *Reichskristallnacht*. Historian Ian Kershaw has written that the "road to Auschwitz was built by hate, but paved with indifference." It was no longer necessary after 1941 to publicize the "threats" posed by Jews, and as a result the Jewish Question became of no more than marginal importance in the formation of popular opinion within the Third Reich. Propaganda had helped to create such apathy and indifference by persuading people that they could retreat into the safety of their private lives and leave the solutions to such "problems" to others. Tragically, the moral ambiguity that characterized the public's response to the well-publicized plans to exterminate Jews and other "inferior" races encouraged the regime to realize the unthinkable.

According to George Mosse, "a myth is the strongest belief held by the group, and its adherents feel themselves to be an army of truth fighting an army of evil." Goebbels maintained that the purpose of propaganda was to persuade the audience to believe in the viewpoint expressed by the propagandist. But if propaganda is to be effective it must, in a sense, always preach to those who are already partially converted. The Nazi attitude to the Jews is an excellent example of this facet of propaganda. It cannot be argued rationally that anti-Semitism was a result of National Socialism or that Goebbels's propaganda made Germans anti-Semitic; but the fact remains that the Third Reich was responsible for attempting a genocide of unparalleled scope and brutality. This situation may be attributed partly to the effects of propaganda itself and partly also to the closed political environment within which that propaganda was necessarily working. Thus, when Hitler came to power, he needed the Jews as a permanent scapegoat on which those in the movement could work off their resentment; the Jew was manipulated to fulfil a psychological need. Nazi propaganda simply used the historical predisposition of the audience toward an anti-Semitic explanation for Germany's cultural, economic, and political grievances. The appeal of *Völkisch* thought was very much linked to its projection of stereotypes—of its own image and the image it created of those who opposed its doctrine or did not correspond to its racial dogma. The importance of the image of the Jew was defined in antithesis to Nazi ideology. The Jewish stereotype thus provided the focal point for the feelings of aggression inherent in the ideology. The whole purpose of anti-Semitic propaganda was to reinforce such beliefs and prejudices and to unify the people into the desired thoughts and actions. The Jew provided an escape valve from serious social and political problems. The "image" of the Jew portrayed in the mass media—and particularly the stereotype disseminated in *Der ewige Jude*—was outside the range of rational intellectual analysis, and that was its strength. In this way, anti-Semitic propaganda was able to overcome any doubts that may have existed, while at the same time providing the emotional basis for a totalitarian solution to the country's problems.

Anti-Japanese Propaganda in the United States

As we have seen, *Prelude to War* (Document 4), was the first of Frank Capra's series of seven documentary films in the *Why We Fight* series. These films, produced for the American armed forces, were supplemented by the *Know Your Ally* and *Know Your Enemy* series. *Prelude to War* pointed to the Japanese invasion of Manchuria in 1931 as the start of World War II: "Remember that date: September 18, 1931, a date you should remember as well as December 7, 1941. For on that date in 1931 the war we are now fighting began." The Japanese surprise attack on Pearl Harbor provided the rallying cry for war, even more than the sinking of the *Lusitania* in 1915 had crystallized anti-German attitudes. Whereas in World War II, the German enemy in Europe was depicted by the United States as an evil regime (Italy rarely figured as a major threat in U.S. propaganda), in Asia, the enemy was depicted as an entire race. In Europe, the United States fought to defend its allies against a Nazi expansionist regime motivated by a racist utopian ideology. In the Pacific War, Japanese expansion was also accompanied by a belief of racial superiority, but American propaganda was itself driven by hatred of the "subhuman Jap." (The Australian government's Department of Information launched a similar "Know Your Enemy" campaign, which was characterized by highly emotional appeals and crude racial stereotypes that demonized the Japanese.) In April 1942, the Intelligence Bureau of the Office of Facts and Figures (OFF) included the following question in one of its surveys: "granting that it is important for us to fight the Axis every place we can, which do you think is more important for the United States to do right now—put most of our effort into fighting Japan or into fighting Germany?" Overwhelmingly, the respondents chose Japan.[2] Such feelings seemed to stem from much more than simply vengeance for Pearl Harbor. They often reflected a preexisting racism, which had been reinforced by the Japanese attack. The animosity was demonstrated in the hysterical and unconstitutional deportation of Japanese Americans from their homes on the Pacific Coast to internment camps, which demonstrated that the Japanese were viewed as an enemy within and without.

Interestingly, the OWI generally sought to restrain, rather than generate, the more extreme attitudes, partly because it was concerned about the negative effects of racially based propaganda on African Americans' support for the war and also because it feared, with good reason, that such blatant evidence of white American racism would be exploited by Japanese propaganda. Nevertheless, "yellow" terminology was the branding of choice when referring to the Japanese, along with depictions of them as animals. They were the "yellow peril" and "yellow monkeys." U.S. war-bond posters variously pictured the Japanese as rat-like or simian monsters, and snakes also figured. But the most common animal was the monkey. Films and cartoons took up the theme without official prompting, with the result that the fanatical Japanese soldier became a familiar and enduring stereotype. In several posters and editorial cartoons (notably Arthur Szyk's savage portrayal of the Japanese as inhuman beasts), the Japanese were drawn as monkeys hanging from trees or lumbering around like big gorillas. The image of a subhuman primate was key to devaluing the humanity of the enemy.

Hollywood produced a series of films that dramatized the "yellow peril": *Wake Island* (1942), *Guadalcanal Diary* (1943), *Bataan* (1943), *Corregidor* (1943), and *Destination Tokyo* (1943). Bugs Bunny featured in an episode of Warner Brothers' *Merrie Melodies* titled "Bugs Bunny Nips the Nips," where the enemy was referred to as "monkey face," "slant eyes," and "bow legs." Accessories and paraphernalia with a propaganda theme abounded: patriotic buttons carried slogans such as "Slap That Jap. Fight for Four Freedoms"; ashtrays were sold with pictures of a Japanese soldier in a rat's body and the slogan "Jam Your Cigarette Butts on this Rat"; matchbox labels urged "Hang One—on Nippon," showing a US Marine beating a Japanese soldier; and the "world largest selling comic magazine" featuring Superman encouraged children to "Slap a Jap" (see Document 45).[3]

Document 45

ACTION COMIC (MARCH 1943): "SUPERMAN SAYS, 'YOU CAN SLAP A JAP. . . WITH WAR BONDS AND STAMPS'"

Document

Source: DC Comics, available at: http://dc.wikia.com/wiki/Action_Comics_Vol_1_58.

Analysis

Superman had been used in anti-Japanese propaganda following the attack on Pearl Harbor. Comic covers also featured Batman and Robin selling war bonds to children under the slogan: "Sink the Japanazis with Bonds and Stamps." Superman would invariably appear rending some form of terrible retribution, but in this cover of March 1943, Superman is seen issuing a sort of proclamation hot off the printing presses that legitimizes and reinforces existing stereotypes about the Japanese. In the poster that is being unveiled, typically exaggerated features drawn from stock images of the day. The "Jap" with thick lenses and tongue protruding from buckteeth is being roundly slapped by a Caucasian hand. Superman's clash against the Axis powers on comic book covers following Pearl Harbor reflected the superhero's transformation from a peacetime social avenger to the patriotic defender of truth, justice, and the American way of life.

Many wartime posters claimed that the Japanese had executed captured U.S. servicemen ("The Jap Way—Cold-Blooded Murder"). Such messages played on the pervasive caricatures of the Japanese as rats, apes, and menacing monsters. The message to American citizen-soldiers was to work harder and avoid absenteeism to help the military defeat of an unfeeling and cruel enemy. To this end, the Tokio Kid series of posters proved highly effective (Document 46). As part of the effort by the U.S. Douglas Aircraft Company to improve its workers' efficiency and to avoid waste, the shortsighted and bucktoothed Tokio Kid fronted a poster campaign. The grotesque racial stereotype combined the comic-book absurd with a sense of threat and danger, visible here in the blood-stained dagger. The message here is that workers who rush to finish their shifts are, implicitly, a boon to the enemy.1

Document 46
ONE OF THE SERIES OF TOKIO KID POSTERS (1943)

Document

Source: National Archives.

Analysis

In this particular poster, designed by American artist Jack Campbell, the message is about conserving resources to help the war effort. Created as part of the company's drive to reduce tool breakage and waste, the Tokio Kid (allegedly based on Prime Minister Hideki Tojo) appears on posters mocking American workers for allowing broken drills, cracked cogwheels, mixed-up rivets, and piles of scrap. The message here and in the campaign in general is that workers who rush to finish their shifts or encourage sloppy work practices are, implicitly, a boon to the enemy. These posters were later used by the government to encourage workers in other companies that were involved in essential war production.

Throughout the war, Japan used historical accounts of the United States' racist past to cite the many racial injustices of the country, which were juxtaposed against their own innate belief in Japan's spiritual and racial superiority. Thus, both sides indulged in race-based propaganda, helping fuel a war of mutual extermination on the bitterly fought-over island battlefields of the Pacific. Arguably, the vehemence of such propaganda laid the foundation for the U.S. use of the atomic bomb against the Japanese in August 1945.

The propaganda stereotypes employed by all the belligerent nations to depict their enemies reveal the extent to which World War II was in large part a race war, a conflict that exposed raw prejudices and was fueled by racial pride. How else can one explain that in 1945, a number of "atomic bomb games" were produced commercially in the United States. The object being to tilt the game in order to simultaneously maneuver the bomb into two holes labelled Hiroshima and Nagasaki.

Notes

1. For a more detailed discussion of the film and Nazi propaganda aimed at the German youth see, D. Welch, "Educational Film Propaganda and the Nazi Youth," in Welch (ed.), *Nazi Propaganda. The Power and the Limitations* (London: Croom Helm, 1983), 65–87.

2. Sixty-two percent of respondents chose Japan, 21 percent chose Germany, and 17 percent were undecided. "Survey of Intelligence Materials No. 21," April 29, 1942: Personal Subject File, Box 155, folder "OWI: Survey of Intelligence, 1942." FDR Library. See also Horten, *Radio Goes to War*, 54–55.

3. T. S. Munson, "Superman Says You Can Slap a Jap!" The Man of Steel and Race Hatred in World War II, in J. J. Darowski (ed.), *The Ages of Superman: Essays on the Man of Steel in Changing Times* (Jefferson, NC: McFarland, 2012), 5–15.

Chapter 22

Postscript

A war, which began with a cavalry charge in Poland and ended with the dropping of atomic bombs in Hiroshima and Nagasaki, also witnessed the largest explosion in the use of propaganda in the history of warfare. The expanding mass media offered a fertile ground for propaganda, and global conflict provided the impetus needed for its growth. The far-reaching impact of World War II led to new political and sociological theories on the nature of man and modern society—particularly in the light of the rise of totalitarian police states in the 1930s.

There followed a struggle between mass societies, a war of political ideologies in which propaganda played an increasingly important role. In the democracies, World War II had been presented in terms of a struggle between the "free world" and the "slave world." Democracy had triumphed but only with substantial help from an ally, the Soviet Union, whose leadership had historically denied its own people the kind of freedoms in the name of which the war had been justified in the West. In the years following the ending of the war and the postwar peace settlements conferences (notably Yalta and Potsdam), deep-rooted ideological differences resurfaced. The propaganda battle to "win hearts and minds" that had been waged so fiercely in World War II continued during the period of economic and political hostility between communist and capitalist countries known as the Cold War. Propagandists on all sides employed their own interpretations of the truth in order to sell an ideological point of view to their citizens and to the world at large.

Select Bibliography

Adam, Peter. *The Arts of the Third Reich*. London: Thames and Hudson, 1992.

Addison, Paul. *Churchill on the Home Front 1900–1955*. London: Jonathan Cape, 1992.

Addison, Paul and Crang, Jeremy (eds.). *Listening to Britain*. London: Vintage, 2010.

Agnew, Kate and Fox, Geoff. *Children at War*. London: Continuum, 2001.

Aldrich, Richard, J. *Witness to War. Diaries of the Second World War in Europe and the Middle East*. London: Doubleday, 2004.

Art from the Second World War. London: Imperial War Museum, 2007.

Aulich, James. *War Posters: Weapons of Mass Communication*. London: Thames and Hudson, 2007.

Baburina, Nina Ivanovna. *The Soviet Political Poster 1917–1980, from the USSR Lenin Library Collection*. London: Penguin, 1984.

Baird, Jay. *The Mythical World of Nazi Propaganda, 1939–1945*. Minneapolis: University of Minnesota, 1974.

Bartlett, Frederick. *Political Propaganda*. Cambridge: Cambridge University Press, 1940.

Bernays, Edward. *Propaganda*. New York: Ig Publishing, 1928, 1955, 2005.

Bodnar, John. *The "Good War" in American Memory*. Baltimore, MD: Johns Hopkins University Press, 2010.

Bonnel, Victoria, E. *Iconography of Power: Soviet Official Posters under Lenin and Stalin*. Berkeley: University of California Press, 1997.

Brandon, Laura. *Art and War*. London: I.B. Tauris, 2009.

Brewer, Susan. *Why America Fights: Patriotism and War Propaganda from the Philippines to Iraq*. Oxford: Oxford University Press, 2009.

Brewer, Susan. "Fighting for Freedom: The Second World War and a Century of American War Propaganda," in Welch, David and Fox, Jo (eds.), *Justifying War. Propaganda, Politics and the Modern Age*. Basingstoke: Palgrave, 2012, pp. 218–235.

Chapman, James. *The British at War: Cinema, State and Politics 1939–45*. London: I.B. Tauris, 1998.

Chomsky, Noam. *Media Control. The Spectacular Achievements of Propaganda*. New York: Seven Stories Press, 1991, 2002.

Combs, James and Combs, Sara. *Film Propaganda and American Politics: An Analysis and Filmography*. New York: Garland, 1994.

Connelly, Mark. *We Can Take It! Britain and the Memory of the Second World War*. London: Pearson, 2004.

Connelly, Mark and Welch, David (eds.). *War and the Media. Reportage and Propaganda 1900–2003*. London: I.B.Tauris, 2005.

Culbert, David. "Why We Fight': Social Engineering for a Democratic Society at War," in Short, Ken (ed.), *Film and Radio Propaganda in World War II*. London: Croom Helm, 1983, pp. 173–191.

Culbert, David (ed.). *Mission to Moscow*. Madison: University of Wisconsin Press, 1980.

Cull, Nicholas. *Selling War: British Propaganda and American "Neutrality" in World War Two*. Oxford: Oxford University Press, 1995.

Cull, Nicholas, Culbert, David, and Welch, David. *Propaganda and Mass Persuasion: A Historical Encyclopedia, 1500 to the Present*. Santa Barbara, CA: ABC-CLIO, 2003.

Darracott, Joseph and Lotus, Belinda. *Second World War Posters*. London: Imperial War Museum, 1972.

Dick, Bernard. *The Star-Spangled Screen: The American World War II Film*. Lexington: Kentucky University Press, 1985.

Doherty, Martin. *Nazi Wireless Propaganda*. Edinburgh: Edinburgh University Press, 2000.

Doherty, Thomas. *Projections of War: Hollywood, American Culture, and World War II*. Columbia, NY: Columbia University Press, 1999.

Eben, Martin. *The Soviet Propaganda Machine*. New York: McGraw-Hill, 1987.

Ellul, Jacques. *Propaganda: The Formation of Men's Attitudes*. New York: Vintage, 1965.

Fox, Jo. *Film Propaganda in Britain and Nazi Germany*. Oxford: Berg, 2007.

Garon, Sheldon. *Molding Japanese Minds*. Princeton, NJ: Princeton University Press, 1997.

Glancy, Mark. *When Hollywood Loved Britain: The Hollywood "British" Film 1939–45*. Manchester: Manchester University Press, 1992.

Hawthorn, Jeremy (ed.). *Propaganda, Persuasion and Polemic*. London: Arnold, 1987.

Horten, Gerd. *Radio Goes to War. The Cultural Politics of Propaganda during World War II*. Berkeley: California University Press, 2002.

Jackson, Julian, *France: The Dark Years, 1940–1944*. Oxford: Oxford University Press, 2003.

Jowett, Garth and O'Donnell, Victoria. *Propaganda and Persuasion*. London: Sage, 1992, 2012.

Kenez, Peter. *The Birth of the Propaganda State. Soviet Methods of Mobilisation 1917–29*. Cambridge: Cambridge University Press, 1985.

King, David. *Russian Revolutionary Posters: From Civil War to Socialist Realism, from Bolshevism to the End of Stalinism*. London: Tate, 2012.

Kirkham, Pat and Thomas, David (eds.). *War Culture: Social Change and Changing Experience in World War Two Britain*. London: Lawrence and Wishart, 1995.

Knightley, Philip. *The First Casualty: The War Correspondent as Hero and Myth Maker from the Crimea to Kosovo*. New York: Harcourt Brace Jovanovich, 2000.

Koppes, Clayton, R. and Black, Gregory, D. *Hollywood Goes to War. How Politics, Profits and Propaganda Shaped World War II Movies*. Berkeley: University of California Press, 1990.

Lashmar, Paul and Oliver, James. *Britain's Secret Propaganda War*. Stroud: Sutton, 1998.

W. Lippmann, *Public Opinion*. New York, 1945.

Marlin, Randal. *Propaganda and the Ethics of Persuasion*. Ontario: Broadview Press, 2002.

McCloskey, Barbara. *Artists in World War II*. Westport, CT: Greenwood Press, 2005.

McLaine, Ian. *Ministry of Morale. Home Front Morale and the Ministry of Information in World War II*. London: George, Allen & Unwin, 1979.

Moorcraft, Paul and Taylor, Philip, M. *Shooting the Messenger: The Political Impact of War Reporting*. Washington, DC: Potomac Book, 2008.

Munson, Todd, S. "'Superman Says You Can Slap a Jap!' The Man of Steel and Race Hatred in World War II," in Darowski, Joseph, J. (ed.), *The Ages of Superman: Essays on the Man of Steel in Changing Times*. Jefferson, NC: McFarland & Company, 2012.

Namikawa Ryo. "Japanese Overseas Broadcasting: A Personal View," in Short, Ken. R. M. (ed.), *Film and Radio Propaganda in World War II*. London: Croom Helm, 1983, pp. 321.

Noakes, Jeremy (ed.). *The Civilian in War: The Home Front in Europe, Japan and the USA in World War II*. Exeter: Exeter University Press, 1992.

Noakes, Jeremy (ed.). *Nazism: The German Home Front in World War II*, vol. 4. Exeter: Exeter University Press, 1998.

O'Brien, Kenneth, Paul, and Hudson, Lyn (eds.). *The Home Front: World War II and American Society*. New York: Praeger, 1995.

Paret, Peter, Irwin Lewis, Beth, Paret, Paul. *Persuasive Images. Posters of War and Revolution*. Princeton, NJ: Princeton University Press, 1992.

Paxton, Robert. *Vichy France: Old Guard and New Order 1940–1944*. New York: Columbia University Press, 2001.

Pratkavis, Anthony and Aronson, Elliot. *Age of Propaganda: The Everyday Use and Abuse of Persuasion*. New York: W.H. Freeman & Company, 1991.

Pronay, Nicholas and Spring, Derek (eds.). *Propaganda, Politics and Film, 1918–45*. London: Macmillan, 1982.

Rhodes, Anthony. *Propaganda. The Art of Persuasion: World War II*. Leicester: Magna Books, 1975.

Richards, Jeffrey and Aldgate, Anthony. *Britain Can Take It: The British Cinema in the Second World War*. Edinburgh: Edinburgh University Press, 1994.

Roberts, Graaham. *Stride Soviet! History and Non-Fiction Film in the USSR*. London: I.B. Tauris, 1999.

Roetter, Charles. *Psychological Warfare*. London: Batsford, 1974.

Rupp, Leila, R. *Mobilizing Women for War: German and American Propaganda, 1939–1945*. Princeton, NJ: Princeton University Press, 1979.

Semmler, Rudolf. *Goebbels: The Man Next to Hitler*. London: Westhouse, 1947.

Shillony, Ben-Ami. *Politics and Culture in Wartime Japan*. Oxford: Clarendon Press, 1981.

Short, Ken. R. M. (ed.). *Film and Radio Propaganda in World War II*. London: Croom Helm, 1983.

Speer, Albert. *Inside the Third Reich*. London: Weidenfeld & Nicolson, 1971.

Stacey, Charles, P. *Arms, Men and Governments: The War Policies of Canada, 1939–1945*. Ottawa: Queen's Printer, 1970.

Taylor, Philip, M. *Munitions of the Mind. War Propaganda from the Ancient World to the Present Day*. Manchester: Manchester University Press, 1995.

Taylor, Richard. *Film Propaganda. Soviet Russia and Nazi Germany*. London: I.B. Tauris, 1979, 1998.

Thomson, Oliver. *Easily Led. A History of Propaganda*. Stroud: Sutton, 1999.

Van Creveld, Martin. *The Culture of War*. New York: Presidio Press, 2008.

Weatherford, Doris. *American Women during World War II*. New York: Routledge, 2010.

Weinberg, Gerhard. *Germany, Hitler and World War II: Essays in Modern German and World History*. Cambridge: Cambridge University Press, 1995.

Welch, David. *The Third Reich. Politics and Propaganda*. London: Routledge, 1999.

Welch, David. *Propaganda, Power and Persuasion*. London: British Library/Chicago University Press, 2013.

Welch, David (ed.). *Propaganda, Power and Persuasion. From World War I to WikiLeaks*. London: I.B. Tauris, 2013.

Welch, David and Fox, Jo (eds.). *Justifying War. Propaganda, Politics and the Modern Age*. Basingstoke: Palgrave, 2012.

Welch, David. "'Working Towards the Führer': Charismatic Leadership and the Image of Adolf Hitler in Nazi Propaganda," in McElligott, Anthony and Kirk, Tim (eds.), *Working Towards the Führer*. Manchester: Manchester University Press, 2003, pp. 93–117.

Welch, David. *Persuading the People. British Propaganda in World War II*. London: British Library, 2016.

Yass, Marion. *This Is Your War. Home Front Propaganda in the Second World War*. London: HMSO, 1983.

Index

About the Author

David Welch is professor of modern history and director of the Centre for the Study of War, Propaganda and Society at the University of Kent. His publications include *Germany: Propaganda and Total War, 1914–1918* (revised edition, 2000); *Germany and Propaganda in World War I: Pacifism, Mobilization and Total War* (2014); *The Third Reich: Politics, and Propaganda* (revised second edition, 2002); *Hitler: Profile of a Dictator* (2001); *Propaganda and the German Cinema, 1933–1945* (1983; revised edition, 2001); *Propaganda and Mass Persuasion: A Historical Encyclopedia from 1500 to the Present*, with David Culbert and Nicholas J. Cull (ABC-CLIO, 2003); and *Justifying War: Propaganda, Politics and the Modern Age*, with Jo Fox (2012). In 2013, Professor Welch co-curated the successful British Library exhibition, "Propaganda: Power and Persuasion" and authored the accompanying book of the same name (2013). He has also authored *Persuading the People: British Propaganda in World War II* (2016).